The New Thought Handbook & Prosperity Bible

Successful Habits and Rules for Life

By: Commissioner George Mentz

Contents

Origins of New Thought

Although there is still some debate to the origins of New Thought, people generally believe that "American New Thought" sprang from the works of Phineas P. Quimby or Doctor Quimby in New England, USA in the early 1800s. [i] : Naturally, we can link the concepts of New Thought to Jesus, Sun Tzu, Marcus Aurelius, Plato, Pythagoras, and others. However, after further review of the American and UK origins, there are strong connections with many of the 19th century New Thought authors such as: Thomas Troward, Dr. Charles Haanel, Dr. Warren Felt Evans, Dr. William Walker Atkinson, James Allen, Dr. Christian Larson, and Wallace Wattles with great transcendentalist thinkers such as Ralph Waldo Emerson along with Christian, Mystical Religions, and Eastern Philosophies. Moreover, Emerson even wrote essays on the metaphysical teachings of Emanuel Swedenborg, and there is a direct link between Quimby's teachings which flowed to Rev.Warren Felt Evans who was a minister with the Swedenborgian Church and also a student of Quimby. With Evans and later Mary B. Eddy, the initial devotion to New Thought was used for spiritual healing with a Christian influence [ii] Additionally, one could imagine that the teachings of Swedenborg and Evans were also inspired by the works of Martin Luther and the Lutheran Pietist movement which espoused a personal communion or union with God. [iii] As per the origins of the name, other terms describing New Thought have been used in history such as: Mental Science. Thus, New Thought, Mind Sciences, Mental Science are similar if not the same philosophies [iv] From Quimby to Evans to Troward and beyond, there was a mixing of teachings which evolved into what we know as New Thought today. These teachings include: Christianity, Swedenborg, Socrates, Plato, Aristotle, Mesmerism, Affirmations, Magnetism, Emile Coue, Ben Franklin, Aristotle, Hinduism, Budda and many many more. This integration is also evidenced by New Thought greats like Judge Thomas Troward, Esq. who was a resident of Punjab, India for many years and was exposed to almost all major Eastern philosophies including Islam. [v] Troward's works such as the "Edinburgh Lectures" are still famous today and even referenced in prime time television discussions regarding bestselling books and movies such as The Secret. [vi] Even though Troward was a devout Christian and Anglican, his works clearly reference the ALL of the Universe and how thought relates to the Universal Spirit.

To make a long story short, Phineas Quimby knew much about religion and scripture and some of his direct clients, followers, and believers later fused Quimby's knowledge of hypnosis, affirmations, and animal magnetism into a form of "holistic spiritual healing methods" that could be used with any student to cure "error thought". In the mid 1800s, a great prosperity teacher by the name of Samuel Smiles, MD became famous.

Smiles' influence is probably underrated, but his impact on the teachings of abundance and prosperity run deep in New Thought.[vii] Dr. Smiles work and books had a huge initial impact on Orison Swett Marden, who became America's first true success and self help author in 1894 which blended insights on practical success, hard work and metaphysics. [viii] Within a few years of Quimbys success, you would see some followers of Quimby develop his teachings into a scientific form of Christianity and healing. Rev. W. F. Evans & Mary Baker Eddy were in fact students of Quimby and basically took Quimby's methods and ideas and formulated manuals on healing where Mary Baker Eddy works later became what is known as Christian Science. However, you would see others affiliated with Eddy or Quimby depart from the supposed rigidity of Christian Science and develop teachings that were dynamic and balanced with a focus on "mind body and spirit" abundance which was spiritual in nature. As an example, Christian Larson's books on metaphysics inspired Ernest Holmes to establish his own work and religious mission with Religious Science in 1927. [ix] From New Thought comes many of the greatest writers and teachers of: Success, Personal Development, Inspiration, Human Potential, Spiritual Healing, & Faith. The major denominations that emerged from the New Thought Movement included: The Unity Church, Religious Science, Science of Mind, Divine Science, ANTN Affiliated New Thought Network, and The Seicho-No-Ie Truth of Life Movement in Japan. Some segments of these movements resembled neo-platonic teachings while others heavily embrace practical Christianity or even focused on Oriental philosophies with a particular monistic view including Hinduism. With these fundamental origins in mind, this manuscript will examine select teachings of some key New Thought, Religious Science or Divine Science authors. Instead of trying to translate and interpret all selected works, some of the writings below come directly from the insights of the authors.

Transcendentalism – The Major Influence

Transcendentalism is a metaphysical and philosophical movement that hinged upon the teachings of Ralph Waldo Emerson.

The movement in the USA became very prominent in the 1830s and 1840s in the Northeastern part of the USA.   Many key players of the movement took place in and around Concord, Massachusetts where other friends and writers, such as Henry David Thoreau and Amos Bronson Alcott mingled with Emerson.

The transcendental movement was new in that it had a focus on individualism and creative purpose. Many countries and nations at this time would never allow a person to rise above the class of their parents or family. Thus, the creative individuality of this philosophy was very self reliant.

Transcendentalists wanted people to be independent of society and self reliant and follow their own internal purpose. By listening to our calling, the beliefs of society can be transcended for a higher consciousness and a higher truth. Ralph Waldo Emerson was a leader in the movement, and said in Self-Reliance, that "Nothing at last is sacred but the integrity of your own mind."

Transcendentalists greatly believed in the ability of nature to give one a deeper understanding of life, as Thoreau wrote in Walden: I went to the woods because I wished to live deliberately, to front only the essential facts of life, and see if I could not learn what it had to teach, and not, when I came to die, discover that I had not lived.

Transcendentalists also believe we are all connected to the "Over-Soul." Because the Over-Soul is one, this unites all people as one being.

Transcendentalism influenced new metaphysical groups such as "Mental Science" of the mid-19th century, which later became the New Thought movement. Many in New Thought considers Emerson, Troward, Hopkins, and Swedenborg as intellectual Godfathers of the philosophy. Emma Curtis Hopkins ("the teacher of teachers"), Ernest Holmes (founder of Religious Science), Charles and Myrtle Fillmore (founders of Unity), and Malinda Cramer and Nona L. Brooks (founders of Divine Science) were all greatly influenced by Transcendentalism.

The Twelve Steps of New Thought – Unofficial

1. **All Pervading God and The Beneficence of God** - We teach that God is Omniscience and Omnipotent. God is principle. We teach that God is beneficent and the source of all good. We believe that we all have the right to be connected to the health, wisdom, and peace of God's Universe. Panenthiesm teaches that God is in all and flows through all, but all of God is not present in any thing.

2. **Divine Spark in All** - Human beings are children of God each with the Spirit of God within. All of god's children are worthy of dignity. Our nature is Wholeness.

3. **Cultivate Effective Consciousness** - We strive for maximum peace and prosperity. Our thinking and actions create our experience and results. Our journey and perception is based on our spiritual condition.

4. **Every Person Has Purpose and Creativity** - Clarity of Mindset is our purpose. Anyone of us can transform, improve, and manifest our greater purpose.

   As it says in **Philippians IV**. "Finally, brothers and sisters, whatever is true, whatever is noble, whatever is right, whatever is pure, whatever is lovely, whatever is admirable--if anything is excellent or praiseworthy--think about such things."

5. **Power of Awareness and Contemplation** - Belief Prayer and Meditation bring us in tune with God and our Divine Purpose and Service. Mark 11:24 That is why I tell you, whatever you pray about and ask for, believe that you have received it and it will be yours.

6. **Cooperation with Universal Laws Creates Power and Prosperity** - The Laws of the Universe are Impersonal and Beneficent. These laws of life are divine laws.   Like the law of motion or law of gravity, constructive mind and actions create constructive results.

   Galatians 6:7 ▶ Do not be deceived: God cannot be mocked. *Whatever a man sows, he will reap in return.* The one who sows to please his flesh, from the flesh will reap destruction; but the one who sows to please the Spirit, from the Spirit will reap eternal life....

7. **Metaphysical Empowerment** - We Emphasize the Spiritual and Metaphysical use of Ancient Wisdom Texts. The allegorical interpretation of the Bible or other spiritual texts means that the Wisdom Literature has various levels of meaning where we seek the the spiritual lessons, which includes the allegorical, the moral, and the analytical meanings.

8. **The Universe Wants Us to Prosper** - We believe that God wants the best for his children. We do not believe that God wants anyone to be sick or impoverished.

9. **Redemption** - We believe in the power of atonement, forgiveness and redemption.

10.   **Peace of Mind** - We believe that inner-peace and harmonious relations are a all achievable if we do the work and truly want them.

11.   **Love** – We believe in the power of love. Love begins with self-regard and self-respect. If you learn to respect yourself and self reliance, you will be endowed with greater power to love. Love of brothers and sisters and love of fellow man is our birthright.

12.   **Wisdom** – We believe that all should seek greater wisdom. There are various types of wisdom. These include knowledge, optimized consciousness, awareness, prescience, sensory perception, and the ability to analyze and respond spiritually to any situation.

The Precepts of Mental Science and New Thought.

1.   Our most important quest must begin within ourselves with an esoteric inner enhancement that connects us to the power, creativity, and wisdom of the universe. The inner transformation must be won before looking to external fixes.

2.   Consciousness has evolved instinctively until the 20th Century. Now we have a choice to make intelligent individual mental evolution.

3.   There is One Power and that power can be tapped into if we desire to have an efficient mind and conscious harmonious connection with the Spirit of the Universe.

4.   The Deeper Mind and Authentic Consciousness have the ability to: Master Imagination, Receive Intelligent Inspiration and Intuition, and even develop types of prescience or psychic powers that allow for a higher order of deductive reasoning, thought and action.

5.   The practice of the presence of God is getting ourselves into a consciousness of our oneness and harmony with God or the Universal Life Force.

6.   The true teaching of Master was the divine possibility of human potential "Be ye perfect."

7.   Practical metaphysics says that you can have anything you earnestly desire as we cannot really desire anything that is not already within us seeking expression.

8.   Our potential comes out of an intuitive awareness of our inner potential which is a knowingness with an open heart and mind.

9.   We can learn the power of willingness to impress ideas and beliefs upon our subconscious minds and to take action.

10.   The key is taking responsibility for our thoughts. Our thoughts occur in mind and are enhanced as a result of our attitudes and feelings.

11.   We must work to awaken the mind and allow mindfulness.

12.   Robert Frost writes, "First thing I do in the morning is make up my bed, then I make up my mind."

13.   Words, attitudes and beliefs are an important part of programming your past, present and future. For by thy words thou shalt be justified, and by thy words thou shalt be condemned. " Matthew 12:36-37

14.   How do I want things to be? Who do I want to be? What do I need to be to become the ideal?

   - ** Each day should be analyzed so that you may enhance productivity
   - Each destructive habit can be analyzed and pruned.
   - Distractive thinking should be set aside
   - The highest meaning of the past events should be cultivated.
   - Lessons learned from past experiences should be respected.
   - A healthy respect for the destructive power of certain people, places and things should be honored.

15, The first step is to construct a mental prototype, archetypal idea or mental equivalent. If the imagination is practiced, the deeper mind will work 24/7 to assist you in your objectives in conjunction with your impression of the idea on the creative life force.

16.   Affirmations have power because they are decreed from a spiritual consciousness. From the work we can speak with confidence, constructiveness and harmony with the universe. The law is set in motion with the word and written word.

17.   We must prepare ourselves mentally each day. Each mental seed will bring forth after its kind, feeling and intention.

18.   Visualizations have power when imagined with a spiritual intent and feeling. Any desired result projected on the mental picture screen of your inner mind, will become an emblazoned potentiality.

19.	Judge Troward emphasizes the power of deep and heart felt feeling when engaging decrees, affirmation, imiganation, and visualization. Know with calm aspiration that all conditions and substance is available for the manifestation of your ideals.

20.	Inspiration is created by the WILL and Willingness to receive it. When we are open to Spirit; then, vivifying thoughts, ideas and feelings will flow into us.

21.	Meet the Spirit of the Universe 1/2 way with your mind, thinking, ideas and actions.

22.	Know with constructive awareness that the beneficent abundant universe will present opportunity and solutions for you to act upon the completion of your objectives.

23.	From this day forward, practice mental constructive thinking. Become determined to think and speak in a way that builds your character, beliefs and your reality.

24.	When mind is made up, it continues to exercise creative power and sets to work out the purpose of that intention and focus.

25.	Spirit and Substance work together: Substance supplies something from which a selection can be made and action can be imparted where the manifestation of our future is an expressing of spirit.

26.	Take action upon your ideas and inspiration provided to you to complete your daily tasks and obligations that lead to your purpose and fulfillment.

27.	Spirit creates by self contemplation. What you contemplate as the law of your being, becomes your reality.

28.	Faith is the substance of things unseen. Faith is Focused Energy. Applied faith is a bit of constructive energy instilled into a belief or an idea or even a healing. All things in balance, an extra bit of faith can stack the energy and potentialities in your favor.

29.   If you are determined to utilize your will to make yourself more sick, you can achieve this, but in the same vein, you may use your will and determination to become more healthy, vibrant, enthusiastic, aware, and mindful.

30.   A pure harmonious relationship with the universe is what allows for a cosmic metaphysical marriage. This unification can allow anyone to become a master of their destiny.

31.   We cultivate the consciousness of oneness with God. To do this, we engage Contemplation or Prayer which is the consciousness of the all-ness of life. Contemplative prayer is a systematic, scientific way of expanding our thoughts and getting in tune with the universal flow of energy.   "Be still and know that I am" (Psalms 46:10) and in that stillness, listen.

32.   To cultivate an idea, objective or desire into true purpose, we must be receptive and have a WILLINGNESS to achieve it. Our will assists in the molding of the faculty of imagination rightly.

33.   The subconscious reasons deductively. Our manifest life is a process of becoming, and we can evolve into new excellence or creativity each day.

34.   Consciousness is generator which provides the degree of love, joy, and peace we radiate into ourselves and outward.

35.   While there are many ingredients to the recipes of harmony or prayer, gratitude is a key term as it dispels discouragement and allows for a living faith, flow and effective consciousness.

36.   Your mental and spiritual consciousness will determine your world view. Your world view will dramatically affect your experience and journey. Thus the totality of your daily thoughts, thinking, actions and omissions IS the Quality of your consciousness.

37.	With action and work, it must be in the Here and Now. It must be with focus and contemplativeness. It should not be with anxious thought. If we believe in our purpose and objectives, it will energize our actions and thought.

38.	Each day is an opportunity to take steps in the direction of the desired ideals, higher consciousness, harmony, and higher order.

The Mystic Renaissance – Swedenborg to the 21st Century

One of the great esoteric writers of the Renaissance is Emanuel Swedenborg of Sweden. In his writings, it can be seen that he speaks of an alignment of consciousness.

To begin with, he advocates that you find your spiritual portal within you that connects you to the universal energy. For example, when you close your eyes and you meditate or become mindful, you will find that place within you where you feel super-consciously connected to the world.

Then, after you have meditated, you learn to seek your purpose and your passion or the things that you want or need to do. And, you cultivate that intent, and you back it up with love energy, if you can.

Third, we begin to live rightly and put your spiritual lives first instead of your ego centric life, and try and live to the best of your ability in constructive ways, live rightly.

Fourth, we would be to maintain a simple faith in knowing just by using humility and compassion for others and for yourself. So, you've helped maintain your faith through humility and compassion.

Fifth, be good to others and to yourself.

And, these ideas ahve a lot to do with the golden rules such as: loving thy neighbor as thyself. As a note, if you look at the Bible and you look in the chapter in Luke.   the scribe or the lawyer says to Jesus that we need to love our neighbors as ourselves, and you need to do all you can to live up to your potential for the grace and glory of God.

As an example, sometimes, we'll watch a sporting event and we'll see someone win something, and they're very praiseful to the God of their understanding. A lot of people are living for the glory of the universe, and they're thankful for the potential that they have, and the talents that they've been given, and the ability that they've been given to cultivate those talents.

Timeless Principles – Aurelius – Franklin – Sun Tzu

The pursuit of success is as old as civilization, and many ancient thought leaders promulgated lessons that are still relevant today. Below are some ideas from three of my favorite thinkers: Marcus Aurelius, Ben Franklin, and Sun Tzu.

Marcus Aurelius (121-180 AD)

Emperor Cesar Marcus Aurelius wrote the 12 Books of the Meditations as a source for his own guidance and self-improvement, and they have some great tips for business, spiritual balance, politics, and relationships. Much like the principles of the Art of War by Sun Tzu or Ben Franklin's 13 Virtues of character development, these insights from the warrior-general are designed to help the reader reach his or her potential. Marcus Aurelius was emperor of Rome and was notable among Roman emperors as he was a devotee to the study and practice of philosophy of Socrates, Plato, Alexander the Great and more. Here are the some Timeless Principles of Success from: Emperor Marcus Aurelius (all references are from *The Meditations of Marcus Aurelius*, translated by George Long. Vol. II, Part 3 of the Harvard Classics, New York: P.F. Collier & Son, 1909–14):

1.   Look for the best in life. (Book 10, §1)

2.   Acting with confidence and poise. (Book 3, §5)

3.   Be and live your purpose and focus upon engaging your vision and mission. (Book 9, §19 and Book 10, §16)

4.   Stay in the now and act in the present. (Book 8, §44)

5.   The present is a gift. (Book 8, §44)

6.   We must express ourselves naturally. Use your own style to be excellent but also use the most practical techniques. (Book 11, §13)

7.   Our greatest power is our choice and ability to control our thought - Choose not to be harmed and operate beyond the basic senses. (Book 4, §7)

8.   Go within to develop inner peace. Renew yourself, rest, meditate, and recharge. (Book 4, §3)

9.   Do your job with diligence, energy, focus and patience. (Book 3, §12)

10.   Be aware of the power within you and nurture it. This can include exercise, diet, rest, empowerment, and learning. (Book 2, §13)

11.   Projects can be broken down to tasks and achieved one at a time finishing each part with excellence. (Book 6, §26)

12.   Our every task is to be done in an excellent way and shine like a jewel of great wealth. (Book 7, §15)

13.   Be contemplative in action and listen to others to learn the best ways to respond. (Book 8, §5)

14.   No need to complain aloud or to yourself in mind. (Book 8, §9)

15.   The word attribute can mean to make a tribute, complement others' good works, and find acceptance and thankfulness outwardly. (Book 8, §23)

16.   Joy and memories are created. (Book 8, §25)

17.   Striving for the right view while repressing animal instincts (Book 8, §29)

18.   See past mere appearances. Try and go beyond what is apparent and see truth. (Book 12, §18)

19.   Focus on your purpose toward highest performance results while avoiding blame. (Book 12)

20.   Use what is available, maximize your talents, and take advantage of the things that are provided. (Book 8, §32)

21.   The imagination can lean toward negativity, but a constructive imagination in the now is very powerful. (Book 8, §36)

22.   Your soul takes the color of your thoughts. (Book 5, §16)

23.   Look at what you have, the things you value most and think how much you would crave them if you did not have them anymore. (Book 7, §27)

24.   Live your life as though today's actions will be remembered and you have one day left as a gift. Act and live without haste or sloth. (Book 7, §56)

25.   Change and impermanence are features of existence. Particularly that change is inevitable and that it should be embraced. (Book 9, §32)

26.   Give yourself time to learn something new and good, and cease to be whirled around. (Book 2, § 7)

27.   The Emperor stresses the importance to flow with the Universe and use its energy in your favor. (Book 8, §23)

Benjamin Franklin **(1706-1790)**

Benjamin Franklin was one of the founding fathers of the United States and was a leading author, politician, inventor, and diplomat. He sought to cultivate success and character in himself and others by using a methodology of thirteen virtues, which he developed in 1726 and continued to practice for the rest of his life. Franklin was a wise master, mystic, and much-loved ambassador. Franklin would reflect daily over his actions and character before going to bed in order to improve himself. Here is a customized version of Franklin's virtues of success (from *The Autobiography of Benjamin Franklin*. Philadelphia: H. Altemus, 1895):

1. "TEMPERANCE. Manage your behavior in a professional way."
2. "SILENCE. Speak with both purpose and skill, and only when needed."
3. "RESOLUTION. Resolve to perform with integrity and resolve."
4. "FRUGALITY. Invest in yourself and do not waste time."
5. CLEANLINESS. Respect of body, clothes, or home."
6. "MODERATION. Avoid extremes."
7. "INDUSTRY. Be engaged in activities that are purposeful; minimize unnecessary actions."
8. "SINCERITY. Be a constructive person who praises others; and, if you speak, speak professionally."
9. "JUSTICE. Keep your personal and business relations win-win where both parties benefit. Treat yourself and others with high regard
10. TRANQUILLITY. Be not distracted by the whims of society and focus on building your family, business and your customers.
11. "CHASTITY. Use your charisma in the right areas of your life."
12. "HUMILITY. Remain teachable and right sized."
13. "ORDER. Keep healthy routines with body, mind and spirit. Use planning to focus on building your character and helping people in each key area of their lives."

Sun Tzu (544-496 BC)

Sun Tzu was a Chinese general who is credited with *The Art of War*, a military strategy guide. Its principles are written broadly enough that many of them still apply to non-military struggles today. Below are some of Sun Tzu's timelessly relevant maxims, modernized for today's strategic risk management battles (from Lionel Giles' edition of *The Art of War* by Sun Tzu, 1910, Public Domain):

a) **Laying Plans/The Calculations**

Use a SWOT analysis for any situation or client. Look at the strengths, weaknesses, opportunities and threats for any challenge or situation.

b) **Waging War/The Challenge**

Know what you are willing to invest in each situation and know when move on to the next option or plan.

c) **Attack by Stratagem/Planning Offense**

All relationships should have a vision and mission. You should know what you will say, how to say it, know the environment, and be prepared to answer tough questions.

d) **Tactical Dispositions/Positioning**

Each of us should know the options, choices and alternative for each unique situations to provide skill and diligence into our activities.

e) **Energy/Directing**

Use your personal energy and charisma to help people but also allow your team to assist you in any way that will allow you to be a success.

f) **Weak Points & Strong/Illusion and Reality**

Each client's situation, business, and family dynamic changes with time. Be prepared to assist customers with each new season by maintaining knowledge about your key customers.

g) **Maneuvering and Dealing with Confrontation**

Be prepared for tough people, tough family members, children, spouses, and other non-traditional relationships. Empower decision makers to work with you.

h) **Variation in Tactics/The Nine Variations**
Be prepared to respond to shifting circumstances successfully.

i) **The Army on the March/Adapting**
With new laws and new government rules, all of us must stay apprised of the best education and information using our awareness.

j) **Terrain/Situational Positioning**
Know your surroundings and people. Communicate with them the information they need to make informed decisions or utilize the benefits that you offer.

k) **The Nine Situations/Nine Terrains**
Understand the terrains of Life, Relationships, Health, Success, Business, Wealth, Mind, Consciousness, and Peace.

l) **The Attack by Fire/Fiery Attack**
Use strategic tactics: Marketing, Time Management, Planning, Management, and more.

m) **The Use of Intelligence**
Competitive intelligence and benchmarking allow you to know your competition, know your customer, and know your target market.

As a Man Thinketh by James Allen, published in 1902.

About the book

The title is influenced by a verse in the Bible from the Book of Proverbs chapter 23 verse 7, "As a man thinketh in his heart, so is he."

The full passage, taken from the King James Version, is as follows:

"Eat thou not the bread of him that hath an evil eye, neither desire thou his dainty meats: For as he thinketh in his heart, so is he: Eat and drink, saith he to thee; but his heart is not with thee. The morsel which thou hast eaten shalt thou vomit up, and lose thy sweet words."

The passage seems to suggest that one should consider the true motivations of a person who is being uncharacteristically generous before accepting his generosity - while in the title and content of James Allen's work the passage is in a different context; In the Bible the passage is referring to another person, and in James Allen's work the passage is adopted to primarily refer to the reader himself.

This book is written in terms of responsibility assumption.

The book opens with the statement:

 Mind is the Master power that moulds and makes, And Man is Mind, and evermore he takes The tool of Thought, and, shaping what he wills, Brings forth a thousand joys, a thousand ills: — He thinks in secret, and it comes to pass: Environment is but his looking-glass.

The original booklet, a powerful essay on the power of the mind, is about 25 total pages. As a Man Thinketh is one of the most read books on human potential and New Thought in history.   James Allen was a British author as well as a pioneer of success movement ideas in the late 1890s and early 1900s.

Chapter 1: Thought and Character

Allen writes that **"A man is the totality of all of his thoughts.**   Thus, cause and effect are the eternal laws that govern the results that have emanated from your mental thoughts. According to James, Man is made or unmade by his ideas or the character of himself and can improve his lot in life by thinking rightly or high quality thoughts and by using the best choices of the focus of thinking and ideas (i.e., choosing right action, right thinking and also omissions).

Chapter 2: Effect of Thought on Circumstances

Allen suggests that "The outer conditions of a person's life will always be related harmoniously to his inner state. This does not mean that a man's destiny or results at any giving time are an indication of his entire character, but that those circumstances received are intimately connected with some vital thought-pattern- element within himself.

Essentially, we are what we think about "all day long". Generally, we are each the master of our own destiny based on the quality of our mindfulness, thinking, mental patterns, efforts, and actions/inactions.

Chapter 3: Effects of Thoughts on Health and Body

"The body and it's actions are the servant of the mind. It obeys the operations of the mind, whether they be deliberately chosen or automatically expressed," And that, upon the body, "habits of thought will produce their own effects, good or bad."

Have you ever heard the saying *"You are what you eat"* This implies that you become what you FEED and Nourish yourself with.

The body is the servant of the mind and acts accordingly. It obeys the operations of the mind, it does not matter if the thoughts are deliberately chosen or automatically expressed. When the conscious and subconscious is continuously subject to a bombardment of non-constructive thoughts, the body sinks rapidly into Dis-Ease and lessened health and immunity. In contrast, the mind that is filled with glad and beautiful thoughts becomes clothed with enthusiasm, youthfulness and beauty.

Chapter 4: Thought and Purpose

You must have an AIM or purpose. Something that you EARNESTLY want to do, be, have, or accomplish "above all else". The AIM is your object or objective. If you think about your goals and objective and desires with great concentration and focus, you will be dedicated to success toward your purpose.

"UNTIL thought is linked with purpose there is no intelligent accomplishment. With the majority the bark of thought is allowed to "drift" upon the ocean of life." " Aimlessness is a vice, and such drifting must not continue for him who would steer clear of catastrophe and destruction ."

 "Thought allied fearlessly to purpose becomes creative force: he who *knows* this is ready to become something higher and stronger than a mere bundle of wavering thoughts and fluctuating sensations; he who *does* this has become the conscious and intelligent wielder of his mental powers."

Chapter 5: The Thought-Factor in Achievement

You must desire wholeheartedly to achieve your goal and purpose.

"ALL that a man achieves and all that one fails to achieve is the direct result of his own thoughts." "In a justly ordered universe, where loss of equipoise would mean total destruction, individual responsibility must be absolute. A man's weakness and strength, purity and impurity, are his own, and not another man's; and they are brought about by himself, and not by another; and they can only be altered by himself, never by another. His condition is also his own, and not another man's. His suffering and his happiness are evolved from within. As he thinks, so he is; as he continues to think, so he remains."

"There can be no progress, no achievement without sacrifice, and a man's worldly success will be in the measure that he sacrifices his confused animal thoughts, and fixes his mind on the development of his plans, and the strengthening of his resolution and self-reliance. And the higher he lifts his thoughts, the more manly, upright, and righteous he becomes, the greater will be his success, the more blessed and enduring will be his achievements."

"All achievements, whether in the business, intellectual, or spiritual world, are the result of definitely directed thought, are governed by the same law and are of the same method; the only difference lies in *the object of attainment*."

Chapter 6: Visions and Ideals

Seek inspiration and ideas, and cultivate BIGGER ideas. Think about solutions for yourself and your loved ones. How can you serve the most people to make life greater for all people involved.   Dream big, and write it down. Brainstorm, plan, and take action. Take steps each day toward your most important idea and purpose. Your efforts will yield momentum, ideas and results.

"THE dreamers are the saviors of the world.""Dream lofty dreams, and as you dream, so shall you become. Your Vision is the promise of what you shall one day be; your Ideal is the prophecy of what you shall at last unveil."

"In all human affairs there are *efforts*, and there are *results*, and the strength of the effort is the measure of the result. Chance is not. Gifts, powers, material, intellectual, and spiritual possessions are the fruits of effort; they are thoughts completed, objects accomplished, visions realized."

"The Vision that you glorify in your mind, the Ideal that you enthrone in your heart—this you will build your life by, this you will become."

"The greatest achievement was at first and for a time a dream. The oak sleeps in the acorn; the bird waits in the egg; and in the highest vision of the soul a waking angel stirs. Dreams are the seedlings of realities."

Chapter 7: Serenity

Tranquility and serenity of the mind implies the effective use and maintenance of your spiritual brain power. Like a computer that is bogged down with old files, viruses, and cache files, Trojans which slow it down, your mind must be cleaned, tuned-up and tuned-in to the universal force.

"CALMNESS of mind is one of the beautiful jewels of wisdom. It is the result of long and patient effort in self-control. Its presence is an indication of ripened experience, and of a more than ordinary knowledge of the laws and operations of thought."

"Your Spiritual condition affects your world view, and your world view defines your journey." G Mentz, Esq. 2005   *The quality of your thoughts affect your attitude, your physical well being, and the way you operate among others. Be sure to cultivate and strive to maintain an optimized attitude of thankfulness, gratitude, joy, love, mindfulness, and a desire be your best. These thoughts will transport you to a higher dimension of operative life.*

Quotes From As a Man Thinketh

- Men do not attract what they want, but what they are.

- A man is literally what he thinks, his character being the complete sum of all his thoughts.

- Cherish your visions. Cherish your ideals. Cherish the music that stirs in your heart, the beauty that forms in your mind, the loveliness that drapes your purest thoughts, for out of them will grow all delightful conditions, all heavenly environment, of these, if you but remain true to them your world will at last be built.

- The soul attracts that which it secretly harbors, that which it loves, and also that which it fears. It reaches the height of its cherished aspirations. It falls to the level of its unchastened desires - and circumstances are the means by which the soul receives its own.

- Men are anxious to improve their circumstances, but are unwilling to improve themselves, they therefore remain bound.

- Every action and feeling is preceded by a thought.

- Right thinking begins with the words we say to ourselves.

- Circumstance does not make the man, it reveals him to himself.

- You cannot travel within and stand still without.

- As the physically weak man can make himself strong by careful and patient training, so the man of weak thoughts, can make them strong by exercising himself in right thinking.

How the Mind Creates Your Success —The Path to Abundance

You Have a Birthright to Wealth and Prosperity

The definition of abundance and true wealth is arguably the free and unrestricted use of all the things that may be necessary for you to advance in the direction of your dreams and potential, thus attaining your fullest mental, spiritual, and physical prosperity. You have a right to wealth. Wealth is that basic desire to have a richer, fuller, and more abundant life. We all should live for the equal advancement and fulfillment of body, mind, and soul; there is no reason we should limit our capacities in any of the three sectors.

Many associate greed, lust, and arrogance as a constituent of the rich, and they wonder if wealthy people are truly happy. Ironically, it is poverty which disheartens the spirit in human relationships, including those we love. Poverty undermines self-esteem, confidence, and our outlook upon life. With poverty as a state of mind and life, we are empty to give to those whom we love and care about. Poverty limits our ability to connect to people and the world. Poverty incapacitates giving, which is the demonstration of love and compassion.

Abundance and creation are forms of wealth, and therefore we must get in tune with creativity. When we do, prosperity will appear in our lives.

Creativity, innovation, and abundance will go to the people who flow and cooperate with life and not reject it. Nature has an inexhaustible source of riches. Accordingly, it is natural to seek more from life, and your advancement is vital for your growth. As the saying goes, we grow or die.

With a higher plane and dimension, we can now make forty years' worth of advancement in three to six years, with efficiency.

As an example, the last one hundred years of science have shown more life-giving and technological improvements than the last two thousand years. This is proof that rapid advancement is available with freedom and discipline at your command.

We will now show you the first secret of life. This key to success can be yours if you simply accept the following statement. Just take it as fact, and the world will begin to move with you.

Thoughts and Wealth Creation

How we construct our thoughts and emotions assists in the manifestation of physical forms and our character. Our worldview is also malleable and can be a great catalyst to creation. Positive and negative thinking facilitates constructive or deconstructive results. For instance, the statement "I need more money" lends the subject to continual detrimental thoughts to "need more money." Changing the focus to a goal (having more money) rather than the problem (needing more money) results in a positive perspective. Rephrasing this thought in a positive manner would be, "I will find opportunity that yields greater and greater rewards."

If you conceive of your desire, you can then imagine that your goal will take place with belief, and then, you will be able retrieve the opportunity from the world's storehouse of riches. As a rule, man originates thought; thought turns into plans or mental images in the mind. Man can communicate his thought and mental images into and throughout the world. This creation begins with our thoughts focused within and without. Your mind is the center of your world. Your thoughts, mixed with a thankful heart directed toward your goals, can flow out into the world as creative energy. You mentally picture and believe that your healthy goal is possible. Understand the essence and reasons that you should have this type of result in your life; you envision your desired outcome with specificity. You think of and picture the opportunity frequently, and you believe that you have the type of result that you desire, feeling it and harvesting the emotion of having it as much as possible. These thoughts and a mental practice of visualization will be sent off into the world like a letter of request. If you practice this visualization enough, the desires you have will be met. Truth is your faithful, non-doubting interpretation of your thoughts. Do not focus on failure, poverty, disease, or deficiencies—your truth is health, riches, success, and happiness. Do not doubt or speak against your thoughts and dreams. Keep these mental petitions as faithful as possible while living harmoniously with people, places, institutions, and the universe.

It is the desire of the Source that you should have all that you need. You will begin with a simple desire for some type of improvement in life; a desire coupled with unwavering faith will correctly unfold for you over time. The motives of your desires are important: you want to help yourself and others, and you do not want to cause harm in the process.

You will achieve these desires much more quickly if your motives are not colored with greed, ego, pride, lust, competition, hate, resentment, and arrogance. Your desires must be propelled by love, gratitude, faith, confidence, mental focus, truth, acceptance, creativity, positive expectation, and clear planning, and you should give more love and value than you take.

Desire and Purpose

Desire is the motivating force that rules the world. Even with today's attitudes—where science, philosophy, and religious metaphysics cross paths—most have acknowledged that: finding purpose, natural expression, mission, and one's true place are all major factors in self-expression and spirit-manifestation. Where a person's true purpose is frustrated, reactions take place, and most people are guided and again redirected by their burning desires toward their highest ideal of creativity and function.

To Begin Your Process of Prosperity

Brainstorm on your ideas each day, clarifying in your mind exactly what you want and how you will achieve it. Hold the picture of the moment you have completed the achievement with positive certainty; never speak or think of it as not being possible, and claim the picture of success as a fact and that it is already yours in mind. Keep your mind tuned in to the universal presence and energy by having a thankful heart and grateful thoughts. If you cannot be grateful, then begin to think of your ability to walk, talk, see, hear, travel, and speak. These are the simplest of freedoms to be grateful for, and they are easily overlooked. Good health is one of these simple freedoms we should recognize with gratitude; in doing so, it initiates a powerful, positive outlook. This new perspective connects you to life and your dreams. People will soon sense this new outlook and serenity that you are projecting.

Remember that you must exercise this mental picturing and thankfulness every day for at least a month. However, after a month, you will not believe the difference in your perception of life. Do not be frightened or ashamed to ask for what you really want. Ask for more than you need. The world is full of people to give and receive. Never be frightened to receive—receive with humility, thankfulness, and appreciation. In the final analysis, extreme poverty and self-sacrifice are not pleasing to anyone, and extreme altruism is just as dangerous as extreme greed. Thus, give and receive with joy.

There is a creative universal force from which unlimited abundance flows. It will give us all that we need and desire when we have a pure heart. A pure heart and mind simply means that you do not allow the weeds of ignorance, bitterness, hate, and irritation to cloud and fill your mind. To facilitate a mind of purity, make the profound connection to the universal spirit within by developing a strong feeling of thankfulness for life, love, health, and material gifts that you already have or will have.

Let us think about gratitude and thankfulness. Can you have happiness with a bitter heart? Can you have real faith when you are constantly blaming, angry, and ungrateful? If you think you can be happy with a blaming, hateful, and bitter mind, then good luck. If you want to change to an outlook on life where you feel that all is possible, then keep reading.

Think back and reflect on the times in your life when you got what you wanted and became arrogant or egotistical. After you received some good fortune, you forgot your humility and abandoned your connection to your universal Spirit. You may have given up your relationship with spirituality because you thought you had won the game of life.

In times of good fortune, it is especially important to exercise and practice grateful thoughts. Doing so continues the flow of riches to us and expands your focus. What becomes important to you will come to you and remain with you. If you have doubt and fear, you will disperse fear and doubt.

Gratitude will keep you connected to the world and afford you a harmonious relationship with all, because gratitude and thankfulness prevent dissatisfaction. Continue to fix your attention in appreciation for the best in life; fix your mind on health, love, success, and good fortune. Your faith will be renewed and strengthened from your own consciousness of gratitude.

Energize Gratitude

There are many ways to promote greater peace of mind. Generally, there is no better method to increase a sense of tranquility than to cultivate a mindset of thankfulness. A good mental practice is to add a five-minute gratitude exercise to your daily routine.   Think about or write out a list of things for which to be grateful for today. This exercise will brings wondrous results. You may not feel results overnight, but within a month you will feel and see the change toward a positive perspective, which becomes a greater worldview. In addition to gratitude, exercise a ban on negativity for one week. Complaining attracts destructive people, places, and things into your life. Each time you find yourself complaining, touch each of your shoulders with your finger and proclaim, "I am abundance."

If you have trouble with certain negative triggers, then eliminate them. If politics bothers you, then quit reading the paper for a short while. If certain people constantly annoy you, then you should avoid them for a time, too. You are working on yourself, and it is okay to take care of your well-being first. The people around you will be happy in the end, if you rebuild and renew your positive spirit and enthusiasm for life as a priority. This is putting your health first, in this case your spiritual health.

Success Agreement

Your desires should be very specific, and your mental blueprint must be just as precise. For example, you may write out on a piece of paper a personal agreement with yourself:

I, Jane Doe, will have a successful business and I will live in a beautiful three-thousand-square-foot home in the Tudor style near Central Park. I am the best I can be in my job and company, and I am very successful in my position, selling creative products and services. I give the highest quality service and value to my clients. My products and services will have outstanding benefits and will help all of my customers. I do all of these things, work hard, and be persistent in my purpose and labor. I will not give up. People will be glad to pay me for my services because they are a benefit to all. I gladly accept compensation and do what I need to do to receive the payment. I will use the fruits of my creativity to build my business, invest in myself, enjoy life, help those I love, follow my dreams, and live in the home of my dreams.

Send Your Petition to the World like a Request That Must Be Granted

Spend each day contemplating your personal commitment. Visualize the success and form an attractive mental image—moving into your beautiful home, helping those you love, or a bonus check for great work. Mentally imagine yourself in that very moment of completing the transaction with joy. Feel it, gather the emotion, and believe that an outcome (or an even better one) is possible. Moreover, you should know, feel, and see in your mind what you will do when you have the wonderful home or outstanding wealth. Then think how you will live, help others, and serve humanity.

A clearer picture strengthens our desire. If your desire is strong, your willingness to focus on the success and to claim it as yours will become a seamless transaction. Each day you must engage your heartfelt faith to secure small steps toward success. Stay engaged in moving ahead with your goals amid gratitude and faith. After you picture your optimal vision and read your personal agreement to yourself, complete the meditative thought process with words of gratitude: "Thank you for the blessing," "Thank you for expanding the quality of my life," and "Thank you for protecting me and my family." This will complete your exercise. Send this petition into the world like a request that must be granted. Then, you should be ready to receive what you want in any form, or even a higher result.

As for willpower, you need only cultivate the idea of willingness upon yourself. Your self-will should be used to think about precise constructive plans and doing specific beneficial actions. Every moment spent in uncertainty is a waste of time—direct your attention to prosperity. The best thing you can do for the non-believers is to show them that you can achieve abundance and success. Your efforts will be a success if your actions are based in a strong desire where you are willing to go the distance to fulfill it. Do not tell the same doubtful people of your dreams and ideas. If you tell enough bitter people about your idea, their collective doubt or jealousy may weaken and sabotage your energy. Surround yourself with successful people, experts in the field, and people who are encouraging and insightful and working toward a new outlook on life.

Always See the Positive Side of Your Present State of Affairs

Interest yourself in becoming rich in life, and always try to see the positive side of your present state of affairs. Focus on optimistic conversation or beneficial events that have happened in your life. Make lists of things to do and begin doing them one by one. It may take a year to complete, but you must begin somewhere. Do each series of tasks and individual actions efficiently. Don't worry about the past or the future or incessantly moan to others about your difficulties or failures. Focus on prosperity today.

Do Only What Can Be Done Today

Take action today. Write our plans for your future for this year, the next 3 years, and even 5 or 10 years in the future. Begin to do tasks each day to improve your lot in life and help others.   Do your tasks correctly the first time, and you need not fix them later. To do efficient and effective work, you need only to do one thing at a time and to not spread yourself too thin. Focus on the now and make your plans incremental or step-driven. One step at a time, with focus and effectiveness, will virtually guarantee success.

You need not try and mandate an outcome. The creative forces will unfold the correct and highest result for you; you merely need to aim in the direction of your dreams with focus and organize your affairs, so that you are prepared to receive the success and gladly accept the payoff. Overall, action is what will allow you to receive your abundance. Do only what can be done today, and tomorrow you can begin anew. In sum, put the faith, vision, and purpose behind your every action to accelerate the path to your higher abundance.

Find Out What You Really Want to Do and Be! - Write a List of Twenty Things of Interest to You Life's Purpose

You should determine what you like and what you love to do through this simple process. Write a list of twenty things of interest to you; continue adding and subtracting from the list. Over time, you will development meaningful ideas because your higher consciousness will guide you toward your given talents. As a note, your purpose could be to research history or science, to read books, to write articles or books, to develop written content, to draw or create art and graphics, to travel, or to communicate with people. Over time your definite purpose should become more specific, such as "I intend to become the best speaker or writer on the topic of politics or taxes, complete a masters or doctorate in international business, and build the best website for information and links to success literature." It does not matter how you start, just begin the writing process! Remember that a good talent (something you like to do and you are good at doing) combined with desire to become the best in a given field of work will ensure that you will do what you love. At the least, you can become a trainer of your trade or profession and give back to the world by accelerating the learning of children or students in your field. Without being boastful, you must convey the impression to others that you are an exemplarily human being for all who come in contact with you. Impress on others that you can add to their lives; speak of your life and business as getting better and better all of the time. Act and feel as though you are successful, as if you are already rich in life and all your needs are met. Incorporate a compassionate humility that you blend with poise, faith, confidence, and self-esteem. You need only speak when necessary, but your strong character and faithful confidence will attract the best people into your life.

Use Your Present Job Skillfully to Move in the Direction That You Want

If you are in a job and cannot leave it to immediately follow your dreams, then do what you can in the evenings or weekends to hone your skills, plans, and education toward your goal. Use your existing position to move in the direction that you want. There are thousands of people who have their business pay for their part-time education; your contacts at work may even lead to a better or different job. In business, you must also be prepared to discuss your dreams (what you want from life) in spoken words. You should know exactly what you want, and you should be able to clarify and quantify your ideas to others in an enthusiastic way. Be able to ask for and accept what you want out of life. You will need to interact with others who can help you. This process of abundance, harmonization, and advancement will lead others to want to help you. Be ready for them, and be open to forming alliances with others. Thus, your visions, meditations, and requests are traditionally answered by the universal power in the form of other people or entities being available to help and guide you—be ready to tell them what you need. Do not be ashamed to ask for win-win relationships with the people that come to you.

Times Are about as Good as You Allow Them to Become

In conclusion, times are only as good as your mind perceives them. Just when you think you are failing is the exact moment to continue your gratitude, meditating on your goals and action! That moment of doubt is when the highest good for you is ready to unfold; sometimes people call this grace. Even if the result is not exactly as you want, something better is coming to you at the right time and place. Therefore, you are many times protected from a bad outcome or relationship by waiting a little longer and preparing yourself for a better situation.

Thoughts Are Energy and Substance

Our Thoughts, Actions, Inactions, and Omissions Create Our Character

Overall, repeated thoughts become tendencies or habits, willingness and willpower can initiate action, and repeated experiences lead to wisdom. Our combined thoughts, actions, inactions, and omissions are what create the totality of our character. If we desire prosperous and peaceful energy, we must be willing to put out good thoughts, praise others, become thankful, see things in an opportunistic light, and have faith in the regeneration of mind and body. Our every action and thought of goodness is very powerful. Acts of kindness, service to others, and self-development are all extremely powerful energies. Negative feelings are feeble thoughts that are a hundred times less powerful than acts of creation and constructiveness. If we maintain a harmonious relationship with others while keeping a peaceful relationship with ourselves, then life can be much easier. Further, when we are avoiding wasteful thinking and actions, our spiritual energies may maintain their laser focus and power. As with physics, it is possible to neutralize a sound wave by setting up another sound wave of the same pattern that comes from the opposite pole. Therefore it is possible to conjure and visualize ideas, thoughts, and images that can completely neutralize old attitudes. By changing your outlook, you can change your future. Every cause has its effect, and every action has its results, but it is desire that is the link that connects the two. Thinking on a higher level requires a mind that is free, lean, efficient, harmonious, and clear. Gratitude and attunement will afford us the clarity to absorb prosperity and build anew.

A Summary of the Science of Getting Rich Metaphysics

There is a spiritual energy and force in every thought, from which all things are made, and which, in its original state, permeates, penetrates, and fills the interspaces of the Universe. A thought in this substance produces the thing that is imaged by the thought. Persons can form things in his their thought, and by impressing their thoughts upon formless substance (interspaces of the Universe) can cause the thing he they think about to be created. In order to do this, people must pass from the competitive to the creative mind. Otherwise they cannot be in harmony with formless intelligence, which is always creative and never competitive in Spirit.

People may come into full harmony with the formless substance by entertaining a lively and sincere gratitude for the blessings it bestows upon them. Gratitude unifies the mind of man with the intelligence of substance, so that man's thoughts are received by the formless. People can remain upon the creative plane only by uniting themselves with the formless intelligence through a deep and continuous feeling of gratitude.

People must form a clear and definite mental image of the things they wish to have, to do, or to become, and they must hold this mental image in his their thoughts while being deeply grateful to the supreme that all his their desires are granted. People who wish to get rich must spend his their leisure hours in contemplating their vision, and in earnest thanksgiving that the reality is being given to them.

Too much stress cannot be laid on the importance of frequent contemplation of the mental image, coupled with unwavering faith and devout gratitude. This is the process by which the impression is given to the formless and the creative forces set in motion. The creative energy works through the established channels of natural growth, and of the industrial and social order. All that is included in his mental image will surely be brought to people who follow the instructions given above, and whose faith does not waver. What they want will come to them through the ways of established trade and commerce.

In order to receive their own when it is ready to come to them, people must be in action in a way that causes them to more than fill their present place. They must keep in mind the purpose to get rich through realization of their mental image. And they must do, every day, all that can be done that day, taking care to do each act in a successful manner. They must give to every person a use value in excess of the cash value they receive, so that each transaction makes for more life, and they must hold the advancing thought so that the impression of increase will be communicated to all with whom they comes into contact.

The men and women who practice the foregoing instructions will certainly get rich, and the riches they receive will be in exact proportion to the definiteness of their vision, the fixity of their purpose, the steadiness of their faith, and the depth of their gratitude. *Wallace D. Wattles (1910) – Enhanced by Prof. Mentz*

Think and Grow Rich – Philosophy of Dr. Napoleon Hill

The original book by Napoleon Hill was based on interviews with hundreds of America's greatest business executives and political leaders. The manuscript took about twenty years to complete. As stated in the original, great ventures begin with an idea. Ideas are thoughts. Thoughts can turn into real things. What stimulates thought? Desire. Strong desires are the basis and beginning of most successes. A strong desire is usually what can bring an idea into a reality. Take your desire and hone it. Cultivate a plan and refine it. Read it daily and you will begin to self-actualize the concepts and apply the actions necessary in your daily life to move in the direction of your dreams. Napoleon Hill places much emphasis on attitude, or constructive thinking. This constructive attitude and thinking transmutes into faith. Based on his research with the most successful executives, Hill believed that belief and faith are the major forces that--when coupled with desire--can propel a plan into success. He equated faith with constructive belief and effective life force.

Planning is also crucial because most people do not define what they will do or how they will do it in any degree of specificity. Thus, he refers to having a <u>definite purpose</u>. This simply means to seize upon a specific goal or quest. <u>Be very specific</u>. Write it down, hone it, and do it. He also places much weight on education, skill improvement, and continuous learning in relation to your goals.

Firmly establish what you want and write it out in specific terms:

- State what you want to accomplish (the dollar amount or specific thing or attribute).
- State what you will give to earn the outcome (effort, work, etc.).
- Write the date it will happen.
- Sign and date the plan.
- Read the plan daily upon awakening and before going to sleep.
- Feel you have it now in heart and mind.

Strategic Characteristics of Your Plans and Actions

- ➢ Your actions must be persistent, effective, and efficient.
- ➢ Your decisions must be strong and unwavering.
- ➢ You must not procrastinate and you must make and act on healthy decisions.
- ➢ Strong thoughts of belief and faith will bring about change in the future, yourself, and the environment. Feel in your heart and see in your mind that you have the thing right now. Feel the emotion of having it, and give thanks for receiving it.

As for your character, write out another list:

- ➢ Write a description of who you want to become.
- ➢ Formulate a written plan detailing how you will achieve it.

- ➢ Desire, thought, and action will gradually transform your character improvement into reality.
- ➢ Self-confidence can be built on affirmations, gratitude, and faith.
- ➢ Eliminate destructive thinking and negative attitude through harmonious thinking and harmlessness in your actions. Example: Engage win-win relationships.
- ➢ Do what you need to do to improve your mind, body, and soul on a daily basis.

As for the process of meditation, autosuggestion, or affirmations create another list:

- ➢ Find a quiet spot to relax.
- ➢ Read your written statements of desire.
- ➢ Believe in your mind that the outcome will occur.
- ➢ See that you have it already in your mind's eye.
- ➢ Believe that you can and will receive it.
- ➢ Put the statement out where you can see it easily.
- ➢ As such, the only limits to your goals are your state of mind and faith.

Discuss your goals with other professionals who want to help you. This is known as the Master Mind Alliance. We suggests that you team up with other professionals with related goals and expertise to obtain counsel. In this alliance, you give as much as you receive in a harmonious fashion while always supporting the group members with your insight, advice, and help.

Overall, a definiteness of purpose of your plan along with a burning desire is generally what is needed to accomplish great things. When you mix this recipe with constructive belief or faith, you become driven to do what is necessary to succeed and *not* to give up. You believe that *you can*.

A burning desire is something that you really want to do. You are solid in your faith that you can allow your desire to become real. You are willing to sever the past and move forward with the desire, goal, and plan. You are willing to focus exclusively on the project, and never give up. You are guaranteed degrees of success if you do something each day toward the completion of your goals.

You develop a state of mind that is conducive to your desires. You have positive thoughts, enthusiasm, belief, and persistence that are all built on truth. Truth can be perceived in a constructive way or in the form of doom and gloom. We all know that a bitter and negative attitude is not an effective way to live and can actually paralyze you, resulting in failure. As they say, "Realists expect failure and demand to be right." Seeing beyond what is apparent takes skill and practice. When exercising the principles of Napoleon Hill in your life, you will obtain this skill over time.

Do you have trouble with constructive belief? Napoleon Hill wrote about methods in his book that are timeless and were heavily used in the self-help movement in the early 1900's. See other authors: Thomas Troward, Wallace Wattles, Christian Larson, W. Atkinson, and more. As stated by many of these masters of self-help, constructive belief and expectation can be cultivated and transformed into a great asset and strength, which will lead to greater success.

Faith can be induced through several practices or exercises:

- Mental images of success. Picture yourself completing your goals in detail.
- Affirmations (reading aloud the attributes or goals that you desire). This can be applied to your character, family, or business dreams. Example: "I am the best teacher, manager, professional etc." or "I am getting better and better every day."
- Gratitude and thankfulness of heart. Think deeply over the gifts of life that you have received on a daily basis. Cultivate a thankful heart based on what you already have or what you will have. Examples: Home, family, health, and more.
- Remember: Like attracts like. Therefore, attitude and character development are about attracting the greater good. Thus, thankfulness and praise are key to attracting higher good.

Building a Master Mind Alliance Network Tips:

- Develop friends who can give you insight and support who will not fill your mind with doubt or thoughts of failure.
- You should be willing to help all in this group of friends with your insight, skill, and support.
- Meet often for planning.
- You must always speak and act in an encouraging way to maintain harmony.
- Know each day what you will do to move forward with your plans.
- Avoid lack of decision and procrastination, and stick with your decisions.
- Continue to organize, adapt, and strive to succeed.

As for life energy, Napoleon Hill implies that we have many forms of energy. These include our forces of attraction or sexual energy. Thus, concentration is critical to focus all forms of your life energy toward your desires. As you know, if you are focusing your primary energies in several areas, you are, in essence, distracted. To prevent distraction, transmute your: mental, Spiritual, physical, and attraction/sexual energies toward your dreams.

You must detach from too-rigid expectations and flow with life. Be specific in your goals, but be open to something better or a little different to come to you as a result of your working of these methods. Additionally, you must also condition the mind to cooperate with the direction that your want to go by cultivating constructive thinking and action. Thus, do not allow yourself to destroy your self-confidence with fear or self-sabotage. Your new constructive belief, faith, desire, and enthusiasm will carry through to the finish line. You will transcend your old thinking into a higher thought.

Your subconscious mind can be influenced through your actions. Therefore, project the image of success onto the "picture screen" of subconscious mind, using a heartfelt energy. Heartfelt energy is emotional thinking that is tied to your mental picture of success. Therefore, your constructive belief, thankful heart, desires, planning and alliances will allow you to lead a more harmonious relationship with the universal forces. Your gratitude, constructive expectation, and efficient action will bring you in tune with universal forces and allow you to develop peace of mind and effective actions. Your harmonious Spiritual and physical actions will induce your mind and the world to cooperate with you and others will be attracted to help you.

In sum, the Universal Spirit will send you ideas and people to cooperate with you. In sum, the world will create opportunity for you and assist you with your dreams. Napoleon Hill alludes to all of this as the "sixth sense." Through the aid of the sixth sense, you may seek out certain goals, and they may not materialize. However, if you continue your work and constructive expectation, something better will come to you at the right time. Therefore, the Universe or sixth sense will protect you and assist your decision-making process. [x]

Thoughts Are Things by Prentice Mulford – Summary

13 Chapter Summaries Analyzed from the 1908 Book

Revisions and commentary by Prof. Mentz [xi]

Chapter One is focusing on the cooperation of the self with Spirit. If we as students of metaphysics realize that a harmonious relationship with our inner self and higher self is a relationship of peace and success, then our cooperation will allow a fusion with our Spiritual and material life. It is an inside job, and we must clear ourselves on the inside to make for the great good and peace that can fill ourselves and our souls with constructive Spirit energy.

Chapter Two is concerned with our external environment and our Spiritual and physical associations. If we associate with like minds of Spiritual nature, we can excel. Persons who encourage and support our growth are good for our growth and health. Many authors throughout history have advocated researching those whom we admire. Ask for their insight. Learn to be the best by associating with the best. Put yourself in the company of those who are constructive. Act as if you are your ideal. Learn to reinvent yourself and grow toward your desired character and image. Avoid those persons who are destructive. Engage life, stay active, help others, and they will help you.

Chapter Three: Thoughts are things. We think, therefore, we are. We are beings of thoughts and creations. What you think is emitted and sent out from you. Your thoughts attract like thoughts. Through constructive thinking, focus, concentration, action, gratitude, thanksgiving, and praise, these things will be brought back to you. Be very specific in your petitions and desires. You are a magnet for higher good if you project good.

Chapter Four: The courage to think what you want and to take action towards what you want is an ultimate power. This type of control and focus may allow you to see in your mind's eye what it is you want and will do. This type of visualization and mental planning prepares you for each day's actions and work. In the present moment, we can do all we can toward our objectives. We cannot change yesterday or do tomorrow's work. We must use our mind and actions toward today's goals and mission.

Chapter Five: This chapter is dealing with the effective use of our Spiritual and emotional energy. If we live in the past and dwell on what has been wrong in our life, then our present energy is dissipated in favor of the ills of the past. Do not blame your past for anything. You are capable of all things new. Your body and mind can be renewed altogether with continued Spiritual and metaphysical focus. Our emotions are very important. If we use our present days, present thoughts, and visualization toward our desired ideals and mix this with our constructive emotion; then, we can move quickly toward what we want from life. Moreover, we can sometimes move effortlessly towards our True Place in conjunction with the will of our Higher Power. As Mulford states, prolonged grief and self-sabotage can destroy our growth and body. Additionally, resentments, anger, hatred, and self-loathing will indeed attract more of the same into your life. Severing from the past, asking for forgiveness, making amends, doing a self-appraisal and proper atonement if possible will free your mind from self-tyranny.

Chapter Six: Mulford states, "We get the element of love only in proportion as we have it in us." Thus, love is the quality of thought and emotion that will propel us into "peace of mind" and also great success. Love all there is. Focus on the good, the best, the constructive, and the beauty of life. See the best in all there is. See the good that results from the world. Meditate on the people that have been good to you, the creation all around you, the good that happens every day, the inventions for the good of humanity, and the positive happenings around the world that occur each and every day. Learn to love all and love yourself, and love will be attracted to you.

Love is a form of gratitude, harmlessness, peace, kindness, and care. Thinking love and giving love will liberate you into the forth dimension of thought. Think of how you have been blessed, protected, and guided throughout your life. Yes, lessons have been learned, and further happiness, peace, and success may be yours if you stay on the path of Spiritual abundance.

Chapter Seven: Mulford states, "If you in your mind are ever building an ideal of yourself as strong, healthy, and vigorous, you are building to yourself of invisible element that which is ever drawing to you more of health, strength, and vigor." With this being said, thoughts of greater things, thoughts of health, thoughts of harmonious relationships, thoughts of peace, and thoughts of wealth will project into the world and mould your life. Further, people will be attracted to you to add to and increase your world and journey. Health, beauty, confidence, and success are mostly a state of mind. We have all seen an average-looking superstar be regarded as absolutely beautiful. Thus, how we think and carry ourselves most definitely affects how we are perceived and how we feel day-to-day.

Chapter Eight: As you know, freedom is important. Allowing ourselves to engage life while heading towards our true place and right livelihood is fundamentally important. People who relegate themselves to something that they do not want to do for their lifetime may be inhibiting their happiness and their potential service to humanity. As with the birds and other animals, each person must seek out what he or she wants from life. Nobody is stopping you from following your dreams. We are not animals. We have choices and an abundance of opportunity in this world. Ask yourself what you want to be, who you want to be with, and how and where you want to live. Think about the possibilities. Coalesce the choices of jobs, careers, business ventures, and creative alternatives that you have in your present and future. Imagine what a person in jail is limited to. Then, envision all of the great gifts and prospects that you have in your life.

Chapter Nine: Mulford states that, "All things" are possible with God. "God works in and through you." We are all parts of the Infinite Power, a power ever carrying us up to higher, finer, happier grades of being. Good is on your side. God is your partner in life. If you join forces through cooperation and contemplation of your Higher Spirit, then you will believe that only good is possible and faith will be induced through your harmonious and thankful mind set and action. As Mulford suggests, "Christ's Spirit or thought had power to command the elements, and quiet the storm. Your Spirit as a part of the great whole has in it the germ, and the same power is waiting for fruition within you. Christ, through power of concentrating the unseen element of his thought, could turn that unseen element into the seen, and materialize food--loaves and fishes." Never underestimate yourself, never speak with discouragement to others, do not keep the habit of doubting opportunity and good. The word "impossible" may be completely untrue. Impossible is a simple response to what others have forced you to believe. Impossible is a simple-minded response and excuse to doing anything. Rather ask: Why not?

Chapter Ten: In this chapter, Mulford is directing us to the reality of the body and its capabilities. The body can grow, heal, renew, learn, and do great works. However, we must realize that rest and peace are vitally important to this growth and renewal. The body or temple is renewing itself daily with new cells and cleansing itself of the old. When we permit our body and soul to grow, heal, and regenerate, we become more effective each day. Christ said, "Ask, and ye shall receive: seek, and ye shall find, knock, and it shall be opened unto you." What this means is that we can ask in our mind, seek and find what we desire. The kingdom is working with us at every moment to help produce what we need. We should only cooperate with the Higher Power with clarity, thanks, and gratitude to allow these things to be given. We must be ready to receive the gifts of the Spirit in the highest form. We would be wise to allow the gift to be given and have an open mind and heart to the ideal that comes to us.

Chapter Eleven: "Thy faith hath made thee whole," said the Christ of Judea to a man who was healed." Are you ready for a better life? Do you believe that all things good are possible? Can your thinking and your character be transformed toward higher thought and toward constructive thinking of Spiritual abundance? In this chapter, a "childlike faith" is mentioned. If we were to approach things as if they are possible, then would we have a better chance of success and happiness? Become open to that inflowing force of Spirit and abundance. Allow yourself to change for the better, take action, and move forward toward your highest good.

Chapter Twelve: Begin your day with taming your mind with Spiritual and constructive thoughts. Feed your body, mind, and soul with the best food, information, and Spiritual energy. Act, think, and be good to yourself and others. Ask and petition from your higher power all that you want. Hope and pray for the best to happen to all and everyone. Bless, praise, and be thankful for all things good. Empower yourself and your Spirit with love, gratitude, kindness, harmonious thinking, harmless action, and serenity. Your highest ideals will be provided by the Universe as long as you do not resist the gifts of abundance and are contemplative in action.

Chapter Thirteen: New thinking is possible. It is a simple adjustment to the way we use our mind. Try to *not* complain for a one whole day. Try to stop blaming. Quit making excuses for not doing what you desire. Your thoughts and character can be reinvented. You can be reborn. Your mind and thinking can transcend into a new constructive awareness. It takes time and effort, but anyone can do it. We must be persistent. In life or business we must press on in mind to achieve the successful results that we desire. Each day is a new opportunity to engage several successful tasks. We need not act in haste.

Conclusion: We can perform tasks effectively and efficiently toward our ideals and goals. We must see in mind or imagination the thing we plan in its completed form, the system or method organized and in working order, the movement or undertaking advancing and ever growing stronger, constructive, and more profitable. To spend time and force in looking back and living past troubles or obstacles over again, and out of such living and mental action to conjure more difficulties or oppositions, is literally to spend time and force in destroying your undertaking, or in manufacturing obstacles to put in your own way.

There is no need to speak or think of the past. The past has taught us lessons. We may not have achieved what we wanted or have been treated fairly. However, we have learned a lesson and need never to participate in a destructive engagement again. Risks we must take, but our new risks will be calculated because we will be prepared for anything that comes our way. We can avoid certain things and engage healthy ones. All experiences are valuable for the wisdom they bring or suggest. But when you have once gained wisdom and knowledge from any experience, there is little profit in repeating it, especially if it has been unpleasant,

Our thought is the unseen magnet, ever attracting its correspondence in things seen and tangible. As we realize this more and more clearly, we shall become more and more careful to keep our minds set in the right direction on self-improvement. It is our divine right to have a rich and full life with Spiritual abundance. The Universe will send people to help us and guide us. We will accept their help and create win-win relationships where all benefit. What is important to you. You Spiritual and material life should both be important to you. What you make important to you will grow. If you make your family, your success, and your wealth important, all will grow in your life. When you blend your visionary mind, your emotion, your thoughts, and your action toward what you want, you will indeed meet your goals and dreams, particularly if you maintain a harmonious and grateful relationship with your Higher Power.

Continue to make prayers and petitions to your higher self or God. See in your mind's eye what you truly want. Do not be afraid to ask for anything that is good for you and for all. Hold that picture of completed success in your mind. Project it on the picture screen of your mind with sharp and defined clarity. Claim it as yours and thank your higher self and higher power for providing it to you. Be thankful, affirm your blessings, and take action toward what you want. Send it out of your mind into the world with thanks and confident expectation knowing that the thing you desire or something better will come into your life or unfold in your life's journey.

Robert Collier: 25 Secrets to Spiritual Wealth:

1.   Collier believed that the great kingdom was within and ready to be tapped if you chose to do so.

2.   He quoted the masters in saying that we should live life abundantly.

3.   He clearly shows through simple truths that mankind has repeatedly denied possibilities and miracles to be proven wrong shortly thereafter. Examples: Flight, space travel, impersonal uses of electricity.

4.   He suggests that we come from the great Intelligence, and where there is intelligence, there is responsiveness.

5.   Where there is responsiveness, there is the ability to cooperate and co-create our destiny.

6.   The greatest methods of creating responsiveness are to use: praise, blessing, gratitude, and love. Direct these forces coupled with faith toward the desired objectives.

7.   He advocated that whatever we focused on with harmonious, thankful, loving, and grateful thoughts would be expanded into our life.

8.   All of these forces of love, blessing, and gratitude, and such are energies of emotion. Constructive and positive emotion blended with specific desire creates great power.

9.   He brings up the secrets of Philippians IV, and states that if we make petitions to the Universe with harmonious thoughts and emotions, our prayers would be answered or unfold during our life.

10.   Sincere desire is necessary to manifest anything on the Spiritual and physical plane. Single-mindedness of purpose and thought is needed to fuel the actualization of your desires.

11.	One of Collier's favorite topics is the issue of the power of attraction or "Like attracts like." Thus, like energy attracts similar energy of that vibration.

12.	He discusses relaxation techniques to better commune with the Great Spirit of Abundance.

13.	Collier in some writings discusses the poetry of von Goethe. Von Goethe's famous poem states, "Boldness is genius." As such, Collier believes that each idea/action does in fact start a momentum of activity or energy toward any objective.

14.	Thus, action must be engaged, one thing at a time. Work effectively without haste and do things right the first time if possible.

15.	Collier also had respect for the axiom, "Believe that Ye Receive Them." The secret of claiming something in mind before you have it. Collier and many other authors sanction the use of affirmations spoken aloud or silently to convince your inner-self or subconscious of the opportunity and fact of having the thing as real.

16.	Overall, Collier emphasized that having gratitude for something before you receive it is the secret catalyst to Spiritual manifesting.

17.	He implies never to talk or speak against yourself or in a negative way in public or mentally.

18.	Collier completely believes in the use of mental images and visualization as a tool of manifesting your desires. Thus, this law of manifestation allows us to call into our outer world whatever we truly believe in our inner world. See things as you would have them in a very specific form.

19.   We can only obtain what we think we can have.

20.   With regard to poverty, Collier understood that it was a disease, contagious, and causes great and unnecessary harm. Moreover, anyone who teaches people to be unworthy of excellence and abundance does great harm to the masses. This point usually was made to exclaim the unlimited supply of the earth and Universe.

21.   Collier would also point out Einstein's law as a way to explain that there is only one material in the Universe, e.g., energy.

22.   Collier believed that the mind was part of the universal energy and receives abundance from it. Moreover, he believed that ideas were things much like thoughts are things. Ideas should be considered and cultivated and acted upon or set in motion.

23.   With anything you want, you furnish the mental idea and energy of it in mind. Hold it in your mind's eye. This desire will act like a magnet to what is needed for it to materialize over time. The stronger the desires and actions towards a harmonious and constructive objective, the quicker the forces necessary will be drawn to you.

24.   As with all else, *believe in yourself*, believe you are worthy, and be willing to receive the great things in life.

25.   After you have honed any good idea, do things to bring it to life.

Note on Robert Collier:

Through Mr. Collier's studies of applied metaphysics and mind sciences, he implies that things grow in our life by expansion. He refers to the biblical word "kingdom," i.e., "Seek the Kingdom first," as the Greek word for "expansion." Therefore, if we seek, direct, and utilize expansion it will multiply in our mind and life. Whatever is praised and blessed multiplies in our life. Overall, love is the most powerful form of expanding force. Hence, when love, praise, blessings and such are directed anywhere, life will multiply where the energy is directed. He quotes Philippians IV in this lesson also. See Philippians in the Glossary. "Rejoice, Be Glad, Give Thanks." In Collier's 1925 7 Volume version of "The Book of Life", Robert Collier addresses many of these concepts. On page 38, it says, " Man is an active part of this Universal Mind. That he partakes of its creative wisdom and power and that by working in harmony with Universal Mind he can do anything, have anything, be anything." [xii]

An Analysis of the Secrets of Judge Thomas Troward.

Judge Thomas Troward – The Edinburg Lectures

Judge Troward worked in India in the 1800's. His codification or world teachings influenced many of the greatest thinkers of the twentieth century American self-help movement. Troward believed that the world was Universal Mind, and the seed of all things is thought in conjunction with the universal source. To materialize anything, one must think it and develop sufficient desire for the goal, coupled with a clear mental image of the outcome. Further, Troward emphasized developing oneness with the source of all or Universal Mind. As he once stated, "Matter is not an illusion but a necessary channel through which life differentiates energy." Moreover, "The raw material for the formation of the solar systems is universally distributed throughout all space. This raw material can be cultivated by our mental and Spiritual powers."   Thus, our mental pictures are the "attraction energy" that allows original substance to take shape. Your mental pictures, constructive thoughts, and concentration mixed with your "I-am-ness" or "harmonious relationship with the Universal Mind" is the recipe that can allow success.

Troward refers to the Invisible Supply in the same way as Universal Mind. He suggests meditation or quite reflection several times per day or (morning and night time). Other exercises may include relaxation or allowing a mental circle of light to surround you and bless you. Develop one-ness and harmony with the Source of All. Then, you can go over your mental pictures of what you want. Quiet and relaxed contemplation along with visualization and confident action is the desired equation for effective meditation. [xiii]

Steps in Troward's Cosmic Manifestation Process

- Relax and cultivate oneness with the Universal Mind or Source of All. (Recognize that you are part of all and in communion with all.)
- Specify exactly what conditions you desire to produce.
- Specify in your mind what you will do with the results of the desire.
- Concentrate the thoughts on the mental picture.
- Visualize the possibilities with confident expectation.
- There is no need to strain. Peacefully allow your thoughts and visualizations to be pictured in the highest outcome.
- Do your visualizations with a grateful frame of mind.
- Your mental images are specific, but you should be open to results that are even better than you have specified.
- Mentally become open to receive and have the desired condition or result.
- Accept that the condition can be yours and believe that you *have it*.
- After this, go out into the world with your intuition and plans and *take action*, leaving no stone unturned.
- Affirmations can influence your belief. An example is the following: Repeating the word "joy" with emotion and with persistence can allow you to live and feel joy.
- Approaching your goals, actions, and mental exercises with enthusiasm and a thankful heart can be a catalyst to your desires.

Dr. Charles F. Haanel, PhD, Psy. D. – The Summary Principles of the Master Key System in 24 Parts – Circa 1912 [xiv]

Introduction: Nature compels us all to move through life. We could not remain stationary however much we wished. Every right-thinking person wants not merely to move through life like a sound-producing, perambulating plant, but to develop - to improve - and to continue the development mentally to the close of physical life.

Some men seem to attract success, power, wealth, attainment, with very little conscious effort; others conquer with great difficulty; still others fail altogether to reach their ambitions, desires and ideals. Why is this so? Why should some men realize their ambitions easily, others with difficulty, and still others not at all?

1. The attitude of mind necessarily depends upon what we think. Therefore, the secret of all power, all achievement and all possession depends upon our method of thinking. The world without is a reflection of the world within. Harmony in the world within means the ability to control our thoughts, and to determine for ourselves how any experience is to affect us.

2. Our difficulties are largely due to confused ideas and ignorance of our true interests. Thought is energy. Active thought is active energy; concentrated thought is a concentrated energy. Thought concentrated on a definite purpose becomes power. This is the power which is being used by those who do not believe in the virtue of poverty, or the beauty of self-denial. They perceive that this is the talk of weaklings.

The value of the subconscious is enormous; it inspires us; it warns us; it furnishes us with names, facts and scenes from the storehouse of memory. It directs our thoughts, tastes, and accomplishes tasks so intricate that no conscious mind, even if it had the power, has the capacity for. On the spiritual side, it is the source of ideals, of aspiration, of the imagination, and is the channel through which we recognize our Divine Source, and in proportion as we recognize this divinity do we come into an understanding of the source of power.

3. It is our attitude of mind toward life which determines the experiences with which we are to meet; if we expect nothing, we shall have nothing; if we demand much, we shall receive the greater portion. The world is harsh only as we fail to assert ourselves. The criticism of the world is bitter only to those who cannot compel room for their ideas. It is fear of this criticism that causes many ideas to fail to see the light of day.

Exercise: I want you to not only be perfectly still, and inhibit all thought as far as possible, but relax, let go, let the muscles take their normal condition; this will remove all pressure from the nerves, and eliminate that tension which so frequently produces physical exhaustion.

4. The greatest and most marvelous power which this "I" has been given is the power to think, but few people know how to think constructively, or correctly, consequently they achieve only indifferent results. Most people allow their thoughts to dwell on selfish purposes, the inevitable result of an infantile mind. When a mind becomes mature, it understands that the germ of defeat is in every selfish thought.

One of the strongest affirmations which you can use for the purpose of strengthening the will and realizing your power to accomplish, is, "I can be what I will to be." Every time you repeat it realize who and what this "I" is; try to come into a thorough understanding of the true nature of the "I"; if you do, you will become invincible; that is, provided that your objects and purposes are constructive and are therefore in harmony with the creative principle of the Universe.

5. In the domain of mind and spirit, in the domain of practical power, such an estate is yours. You are the heir! You can assert your heirship and possess, and use this rich inheritance. Power over circumstances is one of its fruits, and health, harmony and prosperity are assets upon its balance sheet. It offers you poise and peace. It costs you only the labor of studying and harvesting its great resources. It demands no sacrifice, except the loss of your limitations, your servitudes, your weakness. It clothes you with self-honor, and puts a scepter in your hands. To gain this estate, three processes are necessary: You must earnestly desire it. You must assert your claim. You must take possession.

Exercise: Now, go to your room, enter your relaxed state, and mentally select a place which has pleasant associations. Make a complete mental picture of it, see the buildings, the grounds, the trees, friends, associations, everything complete. At first, you will find yourself thinking of everything under the sun, except the ideal upon which you desire to concentrate. But do not let that discourage you. Persistence will win, but persistence requires that you practice these exercises every day without fail.

6. To be in tune with eternal truth we must possess poise and harmony within. In order to receive intelligence the receiver must be in tune with the transmitter. Every thought sets the brain cells in action; at first the substance upon which the thought is directed fails to respond, but if the thought is sufficiently refined and concentrated, the substance finally yields and expresses perfectly. Finding harmony with the universal power will bring you great power and resources.

7. Visualization is the process of making mental images, and the image is the mold or model which will serve as a pattern from which your future will emerge. Make the image clear and clean-cut, hold it firmly in the mind and you will gradually and constantly bring the thing nearer to you. You can be what "you will to be." You should see the end before a single step is taken; so you are to picture in your mind what you want; you are sowing the seed, but before sowing any seed you want to know what the harvest is to be.

This is Idealization. If you are not sure, return to the quiet meditation or prayer daily until the picture becomes plain. Make the Mental Image; make it clear, distinct, perfect; hold it firmly; the ways and means will develop; supply will follow the demand; you will be led to do the right thing at the right time and in the right way. Earnest Desire will bring about Confident Expectation, and this in turn must be reinforced by Firm Demand.

Exercise: Visualize a friend, see your friend exactly as you last saw him, see the room, the furniture, recall the conversation, now see his face, see it distinctly, now talk to him about some subject of mutual interest; see his expression change, watch him smile. Can you do this?

8. As the one purpose of life is growth, all principles underlying existence must contribute to give it effect. Thought, therefore, takes form and the law of growth eventually brings it into manifestation. You may freely choose what you think, but the result of your thought is governed by an immutable law. Any line of thought persisted in cannot fail to produce its result in the character, health and circumstances of the individual.

The law of attraction will certainly and unerringly bring to you the conditions, environment, and experiences in life, corresponding with your habitual, characteristic, predominant mental attitude. Not what you think once in a while when you are in church, or have just read in a good book, BUT your predominant mental attitude is what counts.

Combining harmonious thought and visualization with the great powers within is where true energy and creation comes from. Place yourself in position to receive this power. As it is Omnipresent, it must be within you. We know that this is so because we know that all power is from within, but it must be developed, unfolded, & cultivated; in order to do this we must be receptive and open.

9. Hold in mind the condition desired; affirm it as an already existing fact. This indicates the value of a powerful affirmation. By constant repetition it becomes a part of ourselves. We are actually changing ourselves; are making ourselves what we want to be.

To think correctly, accurately, we must know the "Truth." We must realize that truth is the vital principle of the Universal Mind and is Omnipresent. For instance, if you require health, a realization of the fact that the "I" in you is spiritual and that all spirit is one; that wherever a part is the whole must be, will bring about a condition of health, because every cell in the body must manifest the truth as you see it.

If you require Love try to realize that the only way to get love is by giving it, that the more you give the more you will get, and the only way in which you can give it, is to fill yourself with it, until you become a magnet.

If you require Wealth a realization of the fact that the "I" in you is one with the Universal mind which is all substance, and is Omnipotent, will assist you in bringing into operation the law of attraction which will bring you into vibration with those forces which make for success and bring about conditions of power and affluence in direct proportion with the character and purpose of your affirmation and thinking. The affirmation, "I am whole, perfect, strong, powerful, loving, harmonious and happy", will bring about harmonious conditions. The reason for this is because the affirmation is in strict accordance with the Truth, and when truth appears every form of error or discord must necessarily disappear. You have found that the "I" is spiritual, it must necessarily then always be no less than perfect, the affirmation. "I am whole, perfect, strong, powerful, loving, harmonious and happy" is therefore an exact scientific statement.

Whatever you desire for yourself, affirm it for others, and it will help you both. We reap what we sow. If we send out thoughts of love and health, they return to us like bread cast upon the waters…

10. Abundance is a natural law of the Universe. The evidence of this law is conclusive; we see it on every hand. Everywhere Nature is lavish, wasteful, and extravagant.

The man who understands that there is no effect without an adequate cause thinks impersonally. He gets down to bedrock facts regardless of consequences.

Thought is the connecting link between the Infinite and the finite, between the Universal and the individual. Constructive thought must necessarily be creative, but creative thought must be harmonious, and this eliminates all destructive or competitive thought.

Exercise: Select a blank space on the wall, or any other convenient spot, from where you usually sit, mentally draw a black horizontal line about six inches long, try to see the line as plainly as though it were painted on the wall; now mentally draw two vertical lines connecting with this horizontal line at either end; now draw another horizontal line connecting with the two vertical lines; now you have a square. Try to see the square perfectly; when you can do so draw a circle within the square; now place a point in the center of the circle; now draw the point toward you about 10 inches; now you have a cone on a square base; you will remember that your work was all in black; change it to white, to red, to yellow.

Many fail because, they do not understand the law; there is no link to universal mind; they have not formed the connection. The remedy is a conscious recognition of the law of attraction with the intention of bringing the best into existence for a definite purpose. If done rightly, thought will correlate with its object (what you want) and bring it into manifestation, because thought is a product of the spiritual man, and spirit is the creative Principle of the Universe.

11. While every effect is the result of a cause, the effect in turn becomes a cause, which creates other effects, which in turn create still other causes; so that when you put the law of attraction into operation you must remember that you are starting a train of causation for good or otherwise which may have endless possibilities. We are first to believe that our desire has already been fulfilled, its accomplishment will then follow. This is a concise direction for making use of the creative power of thought by impressing on the Universal subjective mind, the particular thing which we desire as an already existing fact.

This conception is also elaborated upon by Swedenborg in his doctrine of correspondences; and a still greater teacher has said, "What things soever ye desire, when ye pray, believe that ye receive them, and ye shall have them." (Mark 11:24) The difference of the tenses in this passage is remarkable. "Faith is the substance of things hoped for, the evidence of things unseen." The Law of Attraction is the Law by which Faith is brought into manifestation. This law has eliminated the elements of uncertainty and caprice from men's lives and substituted law, reason, and certitude.

Exercise: Concentrate on the quotation taken from the Bible, "Whatsoever things ye desire, when ye pray, believe that ye receive them and ye shall have them"; notice that there is no limitation, "Whatsoever things" is very definite and implies that the only limitation which is placed upon us in our ability to think, to be equal to the occasion, to rise to the emergency, to remember that Faith is not a shadow, but a substance, "the substance of things hoped for, the evidence of things not seen."

12. "You must first have the knowledge of your power; second, the courage to dare; third, the faith to do." It is the combination of Thought and Love which forms the irresistible force, called the law of attraction. All natural laws are irresistible, the law of Gravitation, or Electricity, or any other law operates with mathematical exactitude.

The intention governs the attention. Things are created in the mental or spiritual world before they appear in the outward act or event by the simple process of governing our thought forces today, we help create the events which will come into our lives in the future, perhaps even tomorrow.

Exercise: Get into the same relaxed state in the same position as you were previously; let go, both mentally and physically; always do this; never try to do any mental work under pressure; see that there are no tense muscles or nerves, that you are entirely comfortable. Now realize your unity with omnipotence; get into touch with this power, come into a deep and vital understanding, appreciation, and realization of the fact that your ability to think is your ability to act upon the Universal Mind, and bring it into manifestation, realize that it will meet any and every requirement; that you have exactly the same potential ability which any individual ever did have or ever will have, because each is but an expression or manifestation of the One, all are parts of the whole, there is no difference in kind or quality, the only difference being one of degree.

13. Part Thirteen which follows tells why the dreams of the dreamer come true. It explains the law of causation by which dreamers, inventors, authors, financiers, bring about the realization of their desires. It explains the law by which the thing pictured upon our mind eventually becomes our own. Every individual who ever advanced a new idea, whether a Columbus, a Darwin, a Galileo, a Fulton or an Emerson, was subjected to ridicule or persecution; so that this objection should receive no serious consideration; but, on the contrary, we should carefully consider every fact which is brought to our attention; by doing this we will more readily ascertain the law upon which it is based.

In creating a Mental Image or an Ideal, we are projecting a thought into the Universal Substance (The Whole) from which all things are created. This means that recognition of Universal Substance brings about realization and a connection. When this tremendous fact begins to permeate your consciousness, when you really come into a realization of the fact that you (not your body, but the Ego), the "I," the spirit which thinks is an integral part of the great whole, that it is the same in substance, in quality, in kind, that the Creator could create nothing different from Himself, you will also be able to say, "The Father and I are one" and you will come into an understanding of the beauty, the grandeur, & the transcendental opportunities which have been placed at your disposal.

Exercise: Make use of the principle, recognize the fact that you are a part of the whole, and that a part must be the same in kind and quality as the whole; the only difference there can possibly by, is in degree. If connected and in tune, then your thoughts are mind are in fact heard and received by Creation.

14. Thought is a spiritual activity and is therefore endowed with creative power. This does not mean that some thought is creative, but that all thought is creative. Mankind is part of all there is. Our mind is connected to our body and to Spirit. Each cell is born, reproduces itself, dies and is absorbed. The maintenance of health and life itself depends upon the constant regeneration of these cells.

This change or growth of thought or enhancement of your mental attitude will not only bring you the material things which are necessary for your highest and best welfare, but will bring health and harmonious conditions generally. Imagine over time that your body, organs, and cells being are being regenerated to perfection and the old cells being cast away. In the same way, your power to attract the best from the world may operate if you are harmonious in mind, constructive in word and deed, and into action.

Exercise: Concentrate on Harmony, and when I say concentrate, I mean all that the word implies; concentrate so deeply, so earnestly, that you will be conscious of nothing but harmony. Remember, we learn by doing. Reading these lessons will get you nowhere. It is in the practical application that the value consists.

15. Difficulties and obstacles, indicate that we are either refusing to let go of what we no longer need, or refusing to accept what we require. Haanel gives a scientific example of a tiny parasite that adapts and grows wings rather than dying. In this way, people always have the inclination to adapt,

improve and innovate. The question is when and how? Unfortunately, many times we are taught the same harmful lesson over and over until we are forced to take risk and truly change. To truly change, we must alter mind and spirit with our thoughts. In order to possess vitality, thought must be impregnated with love. Love is a product of the emotions. Therefore, thought and constructive emotion such as: Love, Gratitude, Faith and even Hope will most certainly stimulate the forces of the universe to assist you in your journey. This leads to the inevitable conclusion that if we wish to express abundance in our lives, we can afford to think abundance only, and as words are only thoughts taking form, we must be especially careful to use nothing but constructive and harmonious language, which when finally crystallized into objective forms, will prove to our advantage. This wonderful power of clothing thoughts in the form of words is what differentiates man from the rest of the animal kingdom. Words are thoughts and are therefore an invisible and invincible power which will finally objectify themselves in the form they are given. Overall, we may use constructive thinking and speech to master our destiny. To overcome error thoughts, we may use a conscious realization of the fact that Truth invariably destroys error. We do not have to laboriously shovel the darkness out; all that is necessary is to turn on the light. The same principle applies to every form of negative thought.

Exercise: Concentrate on Insight; take your accustomed relaxed position and focus the thought on the fact that to have a knowledge of the creative power of thought does not mean to possess the art of thinking. Let the thought dwell on the fact that knowledge does not apply itself. Our actions are not governed by knowledge, but by custom, precedent and habit. i.e.

(Mental and Physical). That the only way we can get ourselves to apply knowledge is by a determined conscious effort. Call to mind the fact that knowledge unused passes from the mind, that the value of the information is in the application of the principle; continue this line of thought until you gain sufficient insight to formulate a definite program for applying this principle to your own particular problem.

16. Wealth should then never be desired as an end, but simply as a means of accomplishing an end. Success is contingent upon a higher goal ideal than the mere accumulation of riches, and he who aspires to such success must formulate an ideal for which he is willing to strive. Therefore, the essence of what we will do with wealth must be codified into a purpose of mind and desire. Haanel poses this question to a multi-millionaire with a railroad empire…. "Did you actually vision to yourself the whole thing? I mean, did you, or could you, really close your eyes and see the tracks? And the trains running? And hear the whistles blowing? Did you go as far as that?" "Yes." "How clearly?" "Very clearly."

Visualization must, of course, be directed by the will; we are to visualize exactly what we want; we must be careful not to let the imagination run riot. Thought is the plastic material with which we build images of our growing conception of life. Use determines its existence. We can form our own mental images, through our own interior processes of thought regardless of the thoughts of others, regardless of exterior conditions, regardless of environment of every kind, and it is by the exercise of this power that we can control our own destiny, body, mind and soul. The result will depend upon the mental images from which it emanates; this will depend upon the depth of the impression, the predominance of the idea, the clarity of the vision, the boldness of the image.

Exercise: Try to bring yourself to a realization of the important fact that harmony and happiness are states of consciousness and do not depend upon the possession of things. Things are effects and come as a consequence of correct mental states. So that if we desire material possession of any kind our chief concern should be to acquire the mental attitude which will bring about the result desired. This mental attitude is brought about by a realization of our spiritual nature and our unity with the Universal Mind which is the substance of all things. This realization will bring about everything which is necessary for our complete enjoyment. This is scientific or correct thinking. When we succeed in bringing about this mental attitude it is comparatively easy to realize our desire as an already accomplished fact; when we can do this we shall have found the "Truth" which makes us "free" from every lack or limitation of any kind.

Haanel: "Scientific thinking is a recognition of the creative nature of spiritual energy and our ability to control it."

17. We are accustomed to look upon the Universe with a lens of five senses, and from these experiences our anthropomorphic conceptions originate, but true conceptions are only secured by spiritual insight. This insight requires a quickening of the vibrations of the Mind, and is only secured when the mind is continuously concentrated in a given direction. The subconscious mind may be aroused and brought into action in any direction and made to serve us for any purpose, by concentration. All mental discovery and attainment are the result of desire plus concentration;

desire is the strongest mode of action; the more persistent the desire, the more authoritative the revelation. Desire added to concentration will wrench any secret from nature.

Vibration is the action of thought; it is vibration which reaches out and attracts the material necessary to construct and build. There is nothing mysterious concerning the power of thought; concentration simply implies that consciousness can be focalized to the point where it becomes identified with the object of its attention. Always concentrate on the ideal as an already existing fact; this is the life principle which goes forth and sets in motion those causes which guide, direct and bring about the necessary relation, which eventually manifest in form.

Exercise: Concentrate as nearly as possible in accordance with the method outlined in this lesson; let there be no conscious effort or activity associated with your purpose. Relax completely, avoid any thought of anxiety as to results. Remember that power comes through repose. Let the thought dwell upon your object, until it is completely identified with it, until you are conscious of nothing else. Lesson: If you wish to eliminate fear, concentrate on courage, if you wish to eliminate lack, concentrate on abundance, and if you wish to eliminate disease, concentrate on health.

Haanel: "Intuition usually comes in the Silence; great minds seek solitude frequently."

18. Thought is the invisible link by which the individual comes into communication with the Universal, the finite with the Infinite, the seen with the Unseen. Thought is the magic by which the human is transformed into

a being who thinks and knows and feels and acts. Growth is conditioned on reciprocal action, and we find that on the mental plane like attracts like, that mental vibrations respond only to the extent of their vibratory harmony. It is clear, therefore, that thoughts of abundance and health will respond only to similar thoughts. The connecting link between the individual and the Universal is Thought, and Love and Inner Harmony (a powerful emotion and feeling) is what fuels thought into manifestation or cooperation from the universe.

Exercise: Concentrate upon your power to create; seek insight, perception; try to find a logical basis for the faith which is in you. Let the thought dwell on the fact that the physical man lives and moves and has his being in the sustainer of all organic life air, that he must breathe to live. Then let the thought rest on the fact that the spiritual man also lives and moves and has his being in a similar but subtler energy upon which he must depend for life, and that as in the physical world no life assumes form until after a seed is sown, and no higher fruit than that of the parent stock can be produced; so in the spiritual world no effect can be produced until the seed is sown and the fruit will depend upon the nature of the seed, so that the results which you secure depend upon your perception of law in the mighty domain of causation, the highest evolution of human consciousness.

19. In the Moral World we find the same law; we speak of good and evil, but Good is a reality, something tangible, while Evil is found to be simply a negative condition, the absence of Good. We know that the ability of the individual to think in constructive ways is his ability to act upon the Universal Mind and convert it into dynamic mind, or mind in motion. We

have then come to know that Mind is the only principle which is operative in the physical, mental, moral and spiritual world.

Exercise: Concentrate, and when I use the word concentrate, I mean all that the word implies; become so absorbed in the object of your thought that you are conscious of nothing else, and do this a few minutes every day. You take the necessary time to eat in order that the body may be nourished, why not take the time to assimilate your mental food? Let the thought rest on the fact that appearances are deceptive. The earth is not flat, neither is it stationary; the sky is not a dome, the sun does not move, the stars are not small specks of light, and matter which was once supposed to be fixed has been found to be in a state of perpetual flux. Try to realize that the day is fast approaching -- its dawn is now at hand -- when modes of thought and action must be adjusted to rapidly increasing knowledge of the operation of eternal principles.

20. God is Spirit. Spirit is the Creative Principle of the Universe. Man is made in the image and likeness of God. Man is therefore a spiritual being. The only activity which spirit possesses is the power to think. Thinking is therefore a creative process. All form is therefore the result of the thinking process. When you begin to perceive that the essence of the Universal is within yourself -- is you -- you begin to do things; you begin to feel your power; it is the fuel which fires the imagination; which lights the torch of inspiration; which gives vitality to thought; which enables you to connect with all the invisible forces of the Universe. It is this power which will enable you to plan fearlessly, to execute masterfully. This "breath of life" is a superconscious reality. It is the essence of the "I am." It is pure "Being" or

Universal Substance, and our conscious unity with it enables us to localize it, and thus exercise the powers of this creative energy.

Thought which is in harmony with the Universal Mind will result in corresponding conditions. Thought which is destructive or discordant will produce corresponding results. You may use thought constructively or destructively, but the immutable law will not allow you to plant a thought of one kind and reap the fruit of another.

You may have all the wealth in the world, but unless you recognize it and make use of it, it will have no value; so with your spiritual wealth: unless you recognize it and use it, it will have no value.

Lesson: Inspiration is from within. The Silence is necessary, the senses must be stilled, the muscles relaxed, repose cultivated. When you have thus come into possession of a sense of poise and power you will be ready to receive the information or inspiration or wisdom which may be necessary for the development of your purpose.

Exercise: Go into the Silence and concentrate on the fact that "In him we live and move and have our being" is literally and scientifically exact! That you ARE because He IS, that if He is Omnipresent He must be in you. That if He is all in all you must be in Him! That He is Spirit and you are made in "His image and likeness" and that the only difference between His spirit and your spirit is one of degree, that a part must be the same in kind and quality as the whole. When you can realize this clearly you will have found the secret of the creative power of thought, you will have found the origin of both good and evil, you will have found the secret of the wonderful power of concentration, you will have found the key to the solution of every problem whether physical, financial, or environmental.

21. "A Master-Mind thinks big thoughts. The creative energies of mind find no more difficulty in handling large situations, than small ones." Everything which we hold in our consciousness for any length of time becomes impressed upon our subconscious and so becomes a pattern which the creative energy will wave into our life and environment. This is the secret of the wonderful power of prayer The real secret of power is consciousness of power. The Universal Mind is unconditional; therefore, the more conscious we become of our unity with this mind, the less conscious we shall become of conditions and limitations, and as we become emancipated or freed from conditions we come into a realization of the unconditional. We have become free! Thus, prayer, meditation, and focused thought can be extremely effective in reaching your heights.

It is no easy matter to change the mental attitude, but by persistent effort it may be accomplished. The mental attitude is patterned after the mental pictures which have been photographed on the brain. If you do not like the pictures, destroy the negatives and create new pictures; this is the art of visualization. The Divine Mind makes no exceptions to favor any individual; but when the individual understands and realizes his Unity with the Universal principle he will appear to be favored because he will have found the source of all health, all wealth, and all power.

Exercise: Concentrate on the Truth. Try to realize that the Truth shall make you free, that is, nothing can permanently stand in the way of your perfect success when you learn to apply the scientifically correct thought methods and principles. Realize that you are externalizing in your environment your inherent soul potencies. Realize that the Silence offers an ever-available and almost unlimited opportunity for awakening the highest conception of Truth. Try to comprehend that Omnipotence itself is absolute silence, all else is change, activity, limitation. Silent thought concentration is therefore the true method of reaching, awakening, and then expressing the wonderful potential power of the world within.

22. Thoughts are spiritual seeds, which, when planted in the subconscious mind, have a tendency to sprout and grow, but unfortunately the fruit is frequently not to our liking. To remain healthy and regain health, we must increase the inflow and distribution of vital energy throughout the system, and this can only be done by eliminating thoughts of fear, worry, care, anxiety, jealousy, hatred, and every other destructive thought, which tend to tear down and destroy optimal health. It is through the law of vibration that the mind exercises this control over the body. We know that every mental action is a vibration, and we know that all form is simply a mode of motion, a rate of vibration. Therefore, any given vibration immediately modifies every atom in the body, every life cell is affected and an entire chemical change is made in every group of life cells. Through cooperation with our body, cell life and regeneration can be maintained at its highest levels.

Exercise: Concentrate on Tennyson's beautiful lines "Speak to Him, thou, for He hears, and spirit with spirit can meet, Closer is He than breathing, and nearer than hands and feet." Then try to realize that when you do "Speak to Him" you are in touch with Omnipotence. This realization and recognition of this Omnipresent power will quickly destroy any and every form of sickness or suffering and substitute harmony and perfection. Of course we should see a doctor if they can remove an infection and fix a problem. Thus, we should cooperate with all those available who should help us in a truthful manner while also cooperating with our bodies and spirit to heal, regenerate, and reach abundance. You will then more readily appreciate the ideal man, the man made in the image and likeness of God, and you will more readily appreciate the all originating Mind that forms, upholds, sustains, originates, and creates all there is.

23. One of the highest laws of success is service. Service to yourself and to humanity. It is inevitable that the entertainment of positive, constructive and unselfish thoughts should have a far-reaching effect for good. Compensation is the keynote of the universe. Nature is constantly seeking to strike an equilibrium. Where something is sent out something must be received; else there should be a vacuum formed.

You can make a money magnet of yourself, but to do so you must first consider how you can make money for other people. We make money by making friends, and we enlarge our circle of friends by making money for them, by helping them, by being of service to them. The first law of success then is service, and this in turn is built on integrity and justice. Keep in mind, generous thoughts filled with strength and vitality. Giving without expectation will form a vacuum which must be filled. Therefore, the laws of cause and effect will favor you with your sincere assistance and service to others.

Helping Others Mentally: If you desire to help someone, to destroy some form of lack, limitation or error, the correct method is not to think of the person whom you wish to help; the intention to help them is entirely sufficient, as this puts you in mental touch with the person. Then drive out of your own mind any belief of lack, limitation, disease, danger, difficulty or whatever the trouble might be. As soon as you have succeeded is doing this the result will have been accomplished, and the person will be free.

Attention develops concentration, and concentration develops Spiritual Power, and Spiritual Power is the mightiest force in existence. The power of attention is called concentration; this power is directed by the will; for this reason we must refuse to concentrate or think of anything except the things we desire. "Spirituality" is quite "practical," very "practical," intensely "practical." It teaches that Spirit is the Real Thing, the Whole Thing, and that Matter is but plastic stuff, which Spirit is able to create, mould, manipulate, and fashion to its will. Spirituality is the most "practical" thing in the world -- the only really and absolutely "practical" thing that there is!

Exercise: Concentrate on the fact that man is not a body with a spirit, but a spirit with a body, and that it is for this reason that his desires are incapable of any permanent satisfaction in anything not spiritual. Money is therefore of no value except to bring about the conditions which we desire, and these conditions are necessarily harmonious. Harmonious conditions necessitate sufficient supply, so that if there appears to be any lack, we should realize that the idea or soul of money is service, and as this thought takes form, channels of supply will be opened, and you will have the satisfaction of knowing that spiritual methods are entirely practical.

24. If you have practiced each of the exercises a few minutes every day, as suggested, you will have found that you can get out of life exactly what you wish by first putting into life that which you wish. Every form of concentration, forming Mental Images, Constructive Argument, and Autosuggestion are all simply methods by which you are enabled to realize the Truth.

When you master these steps, you will have mastered TRUTH. The method for removing this error is to go into the Silence and know the Truth; as all mind is one mind, you can do this for yourself or anyone else. If you have learned to form mental images of the conditions desired, this will be the easiest and quickest way to secure results; if not, results can be accomplished by argument, by the process of convincing yourself absolutely of the truth of your statement.

The absolute truth is that the "I" is perfect and complete; the real "I" is spiritual and can therefore never be less than perfect; it can never have any lack, limitation, or disease. The flash of genius does not have origin in the molecular motion of the brain; it is inspired by the ego, the spiritual "I" which is one with the Universal Mind, and it is our ability to recognize this Unity which is the cause of all inspiration, all genius.

Most people understand this word "GOD" to mean something outside of themselves; while exactly the contrary is the fact. It is our very life. Without it we would be dead. We would cease to exist. The minute the spirit leaves the body, our bodies are as nothing. Therefore, spirit is really, all there is of us. When the truth of this statement is realized, understood, and appreciated, you will have come into possession of the Master-Key. [xv]

Now, the only activity which the spirit possesses is the power to think. Therefore, thought must be creative, because spirit is creative. This creative power is impersonal and your ability to think is your ability to control it and make use of it for the benefit of yourself and others. The conditions with which you meet in the world without are invariably the result of the conditions obtaining in the world within, therefore it follows with scientific accuracy that by holding the perfect ideal in mind you can bring about ideal conditions in your environment. What is meant by thinking? Clear, decisive, calm, deliberate, sustained thought with a definite end in view. What will be the result? You will also be able to say, "It is not I that doeth the works, but the 'Father' that dwelleth within me, He doeth the works." You will come to know that the "Father" is the Universal Mind and that He does really and truly dwell within you, in other words, you will come to know that the wonderful promises made in the Bible are fact, not fiction, and can be demonstrated by anyone having sufficient understanding.

Master Key System – The Secret Chapters 25-28 – Observations
The wisdom in the first 24 MODULES or Dr Haanel's work must be analyzed in the totality of life's circumstances. Each person is unique with varying talents and abilities, and ALL people have talent and abilities to be cultivated and honed on the mental, spiritual, and physical planes. All persons have a divine right to live, prosper and love in an abundant and creative environment. All things are possible with desire, faith, love, harmonious action and constructive thinking. It should be remembered that these steps below are important in our quest for excellence and peace. Take the best ideas from the list below and use them to improve your life:

1. The use of concentration and focus in your endeavors is vital. "Right Now" is the only moment in time that you HAVE to LIVE and to be of service. Not yesterday and not tomorrow.

2. Waste must be eliminated or transformed. Non-useful mental energies, thoughts and actions should be processed, avoided, or eliminated. Further, the body is Your temple; thus, you should consider the most constructive engagement of activities to revitalize and improve your body, mind and soul.

3. Cycles of growth and life occur. You may go through phases of struggle, challenge, strengthening, and transcendence. Analyze the cycles of your life. Your growth leads to greater abilities, lessons learned, & knowledge.

4. Your body desires "life force". One of the ways to achieve greater life force is through breathing, meditation, and exercise. There are multitudes of activities and exercise that induce breathing, rejuvenation and the building of mental, spiritual, and physical fitness. It is your job to contemplate how to best accomplish this.

5. Staying connected with the source and forces of the Universe requires willingness. This connection also affords you stronger abilities to propel mind thought into the universe through prayer, contemplation, meditation or concentration.

6. The character of your thought is YOU. What you think is your reality. Your perception and peace of mind is governed by the quality and harmonious nature of your thought.

7.   Love and spiritual harmony is the missing ingredient to success. Your thoughts attract like thoughts. Your thoughts and desires mixed with feeling-emotion and blended with love will manifest opportunities and blessings. You will serve humanity and achieve your highest good with the use of Love Energy and Love Thought. Sometimes love energy can be equated with your sexual magnetism also. The good news is that sexual magnetism and love energy can be harnessed and directed into your relationships, success, growth and other areas in a constructive way.

8.   You determine your conscious relation to "ALL that IS" including people, places, things & the universal spirit. Your conscious thoughts are vibrations that surround you and vibrations sent out into the world. Harmonious thoughts will attract people toward you.

9.   Blessings, focus, praise and gratitude directed toward anything or anyone will tend to bring that person or thing into your life. Thus, what you focus on expands. What is not important to you will tend to leave you, and this includes people, things, spirit force, or different types of thinking.

10.   Surround yourself with experts and those who understand your desires. Form win-win relationships. As you give, you will receive in return.

11.   Be aware of opportunities. People will offer proposals and ideas. You must be ready and willing to receive or use them.

12.   Communication is key. Learn to speak, write, and communicate with others about your goals. Learn to ask for help, follow through, and give and receive to facilitate a more abundant life.

13.   Learn to love yourself as worthy of all the good that the universe has to offer. Speak, act and do "AS IF" you are worthy. Do NOT discuss your

past difficulties, faults or other negative circumstances. If you must, do it with a spiritual advisor or analyst.

14. For specific goals and desires, try to relax and imagine the specific desire as you want it, as if you have it, detailing the picture on your mental screen, capturing the emotion, and harvesting the essence of the desire. Feel the joy of fulfilling the desire and love the thought of it unfolding. Hold the thought images clearly and often to further develop your thoughts.

15. Remember that truth can be more than meets the eye. Try and see beyond what is apparent. Sometimes the eventual outcomes of your plans are better that you could have imagined.

16. Action is the catalyst to propel your mental and spiritual advances. As you enhance and advance at all spiritual levels, your intuition and mind thoughts will guide you to do more and more toward the fulfillment of your desires. You will achieve things one by one effectively which leads you to your highest good.

17. Waking up from the 3rd dimensional dream-state world and recognizing you are finally in the 4th dimension of co-creation with the universe is the fruit of our research, reading, and exercise of these principles. You are now master of your destiny in harmony and cooperation with the source of ALL and the universe.

18. Flowing from all of these steps and suggestions, these blessings will allow you to guide and help others. You give of yourself & teach others so that you can keep your flow with the universe and fullness of life.

Codified, Revised and Extracted from the Master Key System by Dr. Haanel. Revisions by Prof. Mentz. [xvi]

Dr. William W. Atkinson - Secret of Success – 1907 - Also known as: Swami Panchadasi, & Magus Incognitus [xvii]

Laws of Attraction

Desire is the motivating force that moves the Will into action, and which cause the varied activity of life, men and things. Desire-Force is a real power in life, and influences not only tracts, influences and compels other persons and things to swing in toward the center of the Desire sending forth the currents. In the Secret of Success, Desire plays a prominent part. Without a Desire for Success, there is no Success, none. The Law of Attraction is set into motion by Desire.   The mental process has aptly been spoken of as "vibrations," a figure that has a full warrant in modern science. Then, by raising the vibration to the Positive pitch, the negative vibrations may be counteracted while positive outcomes will increase.

Desire

We should Desire firmly, confident, and earnestly. Be not half-hearted in your demands and desires – claim and demand the WHOLE THING, and feel confident that it will work out into material objectivity and reality. Think of it, dream of it, and always LONG for it – you must learn to want it the worst way – learn to "want it hard enough. "You can attain and obtain many things by "wanting them hard enough" – the trouble is with most of us that we do not want things hard enough – we mistake vague cravings and wished for earnest, longing, demanding Desire and Want. Get to Desire and Demand the Thing just as you demand and Desire your daily meals. That is "wanting it the worst way. "This is merely a hint – surely you can supply the rest, if you are in earnest, and "want to hard enough. "

Personal Magnetism

People's mental states are "contagious," and if one infuses enough life and enthusiasm into his mental states they will affect the minds of persons with whom they come in contact. Enthusiasm gives Earnestness to the person, and there is no mental state so effective as Earnestness. Earnestness makes itself felt strongly, and will often make a person give you attention in spite of him self.

All of us emit a sphere, aura, or halo, impregnated with the very essence of ourselves; people know it; so do our dogs and other pets; so does a hungry lion or tiger; aye, even flies, snakes and the insects, as we know to our cost. Some of us are magnetic – others not. Some of us are warm, attractive, love inspiring and friendship making, while others are cold, intellectual, thoughtful, reasoning, but not magnetic. Let a learned man of the latter type address an audience and it will soon tire of his intellectual discourse, and will manifest symptoms of drowsiness. He talks at them, but not into them – he makes them think, not feel, which is most tiresome to the majority of persons, and few speakers succeed who attempt to merely make people think – they want to be made to feel. People will pay liberally to be made to feel or laugh, while they will begrudge a dime for instruction or talk that will make them think. Pitted against a learned man of the type mentioned above, let there be a half-educated, but very loving, ripe and mellow man, with but nine-tenths of the logic and erudition of the first man, yet such a man carries along his crowd with perfect ease, and everybody is wide-awake, treasuring up every good thing that falls from his lips.

Attractive Personality

One of the first things that should be cultivated by those wishing to develop their Attraction of Personality is a mental atmosphere of Cheerfulness. There is nothing so invigorating as presence of a cheerful person – nothing so dispiriting as one of those Human Wet Blankets that cast a chill over everyone and everything with whom they come in contact.

Some of the benefits of cultivating a constructive personality are: (1) that they may induce a more buoyant and positive state of mind in themselves; (2) that they may attract cheerful persons and things to them by the Law of Attraction; and (3) that they may present an attractive Personality to others, and thereby be welcome and congenial associates and participants in the walks of life. Another valuable bit of Personality is that of Self Respect. If you have real Self Respect it will manifest itself in your outward demeanor and appearance. If you don't have it, you had better start in and cultivate the appearance of Self Respect, and then Remember that you are a man, or a woman, as the case may be, and not a poor, crawling worm on the dust of a human door mat. Face the world firmly and fearlessly, keeping your eyes well to the front. HOLD YOUR HEAD HIGH.

Latent Powers – Willpower and Desire

Atkinson implies that we can use our will to force ourselves to get into the habit of thinking differently. We can cultivate higher thinking in many forms such as: constructive thinking, enthusiasm, desire, gratitude and more. Given the great, earnest, burning ardent Desire as an animating force – the great incentive to take action, and we are able to get up this mental "second-wind" – yes, third, fourth, and fifth winds – tapping one plane of inward power after another, until we work mental miracles.

Enthusiasm

A person filled with Enthusiasm seems indeed to be inspired by some power or being higher than himself – he taps on to a source of power of which he is not ordinarily conscious. And the result is that he becomes as a great magnet radiating attractive force in all directions and influencing those within his field of influence. For Enthusiasm is contagious and when really experienced by the individual renders him a source of inductive power, and a center of mental influence. But the power with which he is filled does not come from an outside source – it comes from certain inner regions of his mind or soul – from his Inner Consciousness.

Conclusion

We earnestly urge upon you to cultivate this "I AM" consciousness – that you may realize the Power Within you. The real Individual concealed behind the mask of Personality is YOU - the Real Self - the "I" - that part of you which you are conscious when you say "I AM," which is your assertion of existence and latent power. Remember, the "I" of "you" exists independent of the body. It means the state of being "animated," meaning, "possessed of life and vigor" - so that the state is really that of being filled with Power and Life. And that Power and Life comes from the very center of one's being - the "I AM" region of our mind and consciousness. With a realization of the "I" or Real Self, comes a sense of Power that will manifest through you and make you strong. The awakening to a realization of the "I", in its clearness and vividness, will cause you to feel a sense of Being and Power that you have never before known. And then there will come naturally to you the correlated consciousness which expresses itself in the statement, "I CAN and I WILL," one of the grandest affirmations of Power that man can make. This "I Can and I Will" consciousness is that expression of the Something Within, which we trust that you will realize and manifest. We feel that behind all the advice that we can give you, this one thing is the PRIME FACTOR in the Secret of Success.

You can always get a better "running start" when in action, which will give you an advantage over the best "standing start" imaginable. Get into action and motion. We have endeavored to call your attention to something of far greater importance than a mere code of rules and general advice. We have pointed out to you the glorious fact that within each of you there is a Something Within, which if once aroused would give you a greatly increased power and capacity. And so we have tried to tell you this story of the Something Within, from different viewpoints, so that you might catch the idea in several ways. We firmly believe that Success depends most materially upon a recognition and manifestation of this Something Within. [xviii]

The Plentiful Power of the Great Teacher: Dr. Joseph Murphy, PhD, D.R.S, D.D., LL.D [xix]

1.	God wants us to be happy, successful, healthy, and to have a rich, abundant, and full life.

2.	Your subconscious mind has powers that can be influenced by your conscious mind. Consistently making constructive impressions on your subconscious mind will soon change your thinking, your energy, your effectiveness, and your vibration.

3.	Rejoice and be exceedingly glad that the Universe has blessed you, your family, your ideas and actions.

4.	If there is lack in our lives, we need only to think and do something about it to improve our lot in life. Real inner change and outer character may be needed.

5.	Money is only a medium of exchange and a symbol much like sheep or cattle have been in the past.

6.	He believed that money is not the root of all evil unless you worship money in and of itself, which we all know is a violation of the laws of abundance. Peace of mind, balance, harmony, right mind, right action, and right livelihood will invariably lead to richness of life, which includes an abundance of money.

7.	Success and money should be used to constructively serve humanity. Thus, the intention and essence of wealth must be known and directed in a manner that is good for all.

8.	He believed that wealth was a state of mind, and the consciousness of poverty is not useful for anyone and can paralyze the student. Therefore, a change in consciousness to wealth and prosperity can indeed open the doors for ideas, opportunity, and blessings from the Supreme.

9.   He believed that we should commune with universal mind and know and claim mentally and verbally that Spirit can and will bless us into prosperity.

10.   Murphy believes in the source or Divine Mind and is the origin of all wealth. Thus, if we realize and connect to that source, our life and path will be abundant.

11.   Murphy believed that concentrated thought charged with heart- felt emotion or feelings would almost certainly manifest over time.

12.   When man operates on a level of thought that is harmonious and constructive, the Spiritual powers within and without will respond to our mind and actions.

13.   Whatever the mind dwells upon will expand and multiply in your life. Whatever the mind praises, blesses, and is thankful for will most probably increase in our life.

14.   Love is the most powerful feeling or Spirit energy. However, praise, thankfulness, gratitude, and peace are also just as powerful when continuously directed toward an objective such as a relationship, job, or goal.

15.   He suggests releasing your petitions to the Universe. Think it, feel it, claim it, mentally have it, mentally project it on your subconscious picture screen, but then *release* it with a sense of detachment, faith, and confidence where you know that the highest good and outcome will unfold.

16.   Murphy was a strong advocate of blessing those whom we would otherwise be jealous of. Thus, if somebody is doing well or become

successful, then, we should mentally and verbally praise them whether friend or foe. The crux of this strategy is to think constructively without offsetting your vibration with opposite thoughts of envy and character assassination of others.

17.   Murphy agreed with Troward in this way: A person who has seen the end has effectively willed the means (the seed) to the realization of the end. It is up to us to cultivate the seed from that juncture.

18.   Murphy thinks that those who use constructive affirmations and who *know* in their heart with emotion that the affirmation is true, are consciously communing with the divine Spirit of abundance along with changing their individual character and consciousness for the better.

19.   Overall, Murphy believes that man's subconscious or inner Spirit is the root of self-enhancing power and the vital connection to Spiritual abundance. He believes that this part of the being can be affected by certain constructive habits and dominant thoughts. He tries to convey that one should muster the mind energy to will dominant thoughts over self-defeating ones.

20.   He encourages affirming what the heart, mind, and subconscious mind is *willing to* accept and *then* grow the essence of acceptance in that manner to prevent contradiction of mind. Thus, as a newer student of the philosophy, he suggests using statements that you can accept with minimal doubt such as, "I am getting better and better, or my income or business sales are increasing every day.

21.   Moreover, Murphy is also an promoter of relaxing the body, mind, and Spirit before making petitions to the Universe and to your inner subconscious. After getting into quiet communion with your higher self, you

should use affirmations and visualizations with specificity and send them into the world after contemplation.

22.   Murphy uses the teachings of Jesus to emphasize that we do not need to live in the illusion of lack and poverty. There is plenty for all, and the Universe *will* simply create more for everyone when we are operating in the Spiritual dimension.

23.   Engage the mind-set of opulence. Imagine the end result of your short-term or long-term desires. Feel that it is true and a reality *right now* and rejoice in *it. Claim it* as *yours* in *mind.*

24.   Reject what seems to be true that is based only on apparent reality. Try to see beyond what your mind of lack wants you to see. Try to see the good in all and *not* just the inconvenience of a present, past, or future event.

25.   Murphy does state that your outer world is directly correlated to your inner thinking. Thus, we should try to correct any error thought and improve the quality of our thinking and Spirit connection.

26.   We should use prayer or quiet reflection to cleanse our mind and Spirit of self-defeating thoughts and to quit using destructive thoughts or the past as an excuse not to succeed.

27.   As for relationships, Murphy espoused that students should pray for others, forgive others, and develop harmony for others inside and out. It seems that he believes that we will have great relationships when we are spiritually whole, happy and at peace. Moreover, Murphy leads us to believe that we will attract greater relationships of love and trust when we become better and happier persons (filled with self-love) through the Spirit of attraction.

28.   He suggests that we should not allow fear, doubt, and commentary from others or from our own mind to blemish our new and improved mental outlook and visualizations.

29.   As an exercise, stand in the mirror and affirm health, wealth, peace, and success with amazing results. Keep doing this and see how your mind perception increases and changes for the good.

30.   One of Murphy's best exercises is the use of mental allegory. Thus, students can visualize themselves being congratulated for achieving some wonderful result, objective, or dream.

Eight Pillars of Prosperity: 1911 – Summary Concepts of James Allen's Forgotten Book of Secrets. [xx]

In James Allen's Eight Pillars of Prosperity, he teaches us of several keys to success and happiness. Allen believes that prosperity rests upon a moral and quasi spiritual foundation. The foundation consists of the Eight Pillars which include: Energy, Economy, Integrity, System, Sympathy, Sincerity, Impartiality and Self-Reliance.

Energy

Energy should be directed and focused upon what you want to expand in your life. Negative focus can lead to a debilitating daily existence of frustration. Therefore, the concentration of your thoughts upon the best and being your best (in mind and action) can lead to a life of harmonious and effective living. Life will become easier as you are not resisting everything, but flowing with it & making an effective use of your decisions and energy. Don't worry about what was. Focus on what you want to become and how you can help others. Each day, engage in constructive tasks toward your dreams and building high character.

Other key terms to this step are: Promptness, Vigilance, and Industriousness, and Earnestness.

Economy

Economy has been addressed by the greats such as Ben Franklin and also in the ancient scriptures. There is no need to waste your time, energy or money. Making the best of your efforts and constructively use your assets and talents. There is no need for haste or waste. You can be creative and win without hurting anyone while helping many…

Other keys terms to this step are: Moderation, Efficiency, Resourcefulness, and Creativeness.

Integrity

Your integrity is part of your character. Character can be developed to provide the positive impression upon all those you meet and interact with. You do what you say you will do and you do it right the first time. People will soon recognize that you follow through on your commitments and that you are a person of strength, honesty, power, and trust. Further, this habit of following through with your obligations to yourself and others will drive you to be a very successful person. Moreover, avoiding things that are a waste of your time will benefit all persons as you will not engage things that do not improve life for all.

Other keys terms to this step are: Honestly, Fearlessness, Purposefulness, and Invincibility.

System –Planning

Preparing for your goals is fundamental. Plan what you are going to do. Be very specific. Outline the steps needed and drive toward the desired outcome. Be prepared for outcomes that are as good as or even better than you desire. Know what you will do and prepare for any circumstance of importance. Be ready to act, engage, contemplate, and receive your good.

Other Keys to this Step are: Readiness, Accurateness, Utility, and Comprehensiveness.

Sympathy and Harmony

The ability to put yourself in the shoes of another will allow you to develop understanding of others. We do not know what other people are thinking or experiencing. Thus, we try to understand others goals and challenges. Let your kindness and gentleness be known.   Speak and act with power, strength, grace and poise. Do not react to the world, RESPOND to it with Responsibility and treat others in the ways that you would want to be treated. Learn to communicate and receive opportunity by understanding what others are saying first.

Other keys terms to this step are: Kindness, Gentleness, Insight, Awareness, and Generosity.

Sincerity

Honesty is connected to truth. There is the truth that others speak, but more importantly, there is the truth of what we perceive and analyze. When we operate on this earthly plane, we must try to perceive truth at the highest level. If you sincerely act and think in certain constructive ways, vast opportunity will be attracted to you. As above, so below AND "Like attracts Like". You need not seek power over others, you give others the impression of increase and they will be attracted to your value, service, wisdom and quality of your living.

Other keys terms to this step are: Attractiveness, Power, and Simplicity

Impartiality

Sometimes the word impartial implies that we should not keep bias. This less bias that we hold in our preconceptions, the more harmony that we have with the world.   Our minds must be open to receive from any channels of higher good that are provided.

Other keys terms to this pillar are: Justice, Patience, Wisdom, and Calmness

Self Reliance

You are to become rich in life. Spiritual Abundance is yours and it is your birthright. Your sixth sense becomes available to you through your connection to spiritual abundance and prosperity. You are connected and harmonized with the universe; thus, you are cooperating and co-creating with the world. You will become self reliant as you are moving closer to your true place which is utilizing your unique and creative abilities. Your true place is your right livelihood. Your "true place" IS your labor of love, and your career and efforts will be further harmonized to become a wealth of opportunity and abundance in your personal and working endeavors. Remain committed to your dreams & your true self so that your given talents will unfold and multiply.

Other keys terms to this step are: Decisiveness, Independence, Dignity, and Steadfastness.

- Interpreted and extracted from the works of James Allen – As a Man Thinketh 1902 and 8 Pillars of Prosperity 1911 [xxi]

The Mind Philosophy of Dr. Christian D. Larson

To use the power of the mind, the **first** essential is to direct every mental action toward the goal in view, and this direction must not be occasional, but constant. Most minds, however, do not apply this law. They think about a certain thing one moment, and about something else the next moment. At a certain hour their mental actions work along a certain line, and at the next hour those actions work along a different line. Sometimes the goal in view is one thing, and sometimes another, so the actions of the mind do not move constantly toward a certain definite goal, but are mostly scattered. We know, however, that individuals who are actually working themselves steadily and surely toward the goal they have in view, invariably direct all the power of their thought upon that goal. In their mind not a single mental action is thrown away, not a single mental force wasted. All the power that is in them is being directed to work for what they wish to accomplish, and the reason that every power responds in this way is because they are not thinking of one thing now and something else the next moment.

The **second** essential is to make every mental action positive. When we desire certain things or when we think of certain things we wish to attain or achieve, the question should be if our mental attitudes at the time are positive or negative. To answer this we only have to remember that every positive action always goes toward that which receives its attention, whereas a negative action always retreats. A positive action is an action that you feel when you realize that every force in your entire system is pushed forward, so to speak, and that it is passing through what may be termed an expanding and enlarging state of feeling or consciousness.

The principle is to direct the power of mind upon the very highest, the very largest, and the very greatest mental conception of that which we intend to achieve. The first essential, therefore, is to direct the full power of mind and thought upon the goal in view, and to continue to direct the mind in that manner every minute, regardless of circumstances or conditions. The second essential is to make every mental action positive.

The **third** essential in the right use of the mind is to make every mental action constructive. A constructive mental action is one that is based upon a deep-seated desire to develop, to increase, to achieve, to attain--in brief, to become larger and greater, and to do something of far greater worth than has been done before. If you will cause every mental action you entertain to have that feeling, constructiveness will soon became second nature to your entire mental system; that is, all the forces of your mind will begin to become building forces, and will continue to build you up along any line through which you may desire to act.

Inspire your mind constantly with a building desire, and make this desire so strong that every part of your system will constantly feel that it wants to become greater, more capable and more efficient. An excellent practice in this connection is to try to enlarge upon all your ideas of things whenever you have spare moments for real thought. This practice will tend to produce a growing tendency in every process of your thinking. Another good practice is to inspire every mental action with more ambition.

We cannot have too much ambition. We may have too much aimless ambition, but we cannot have too much real constructive ambition. If your ambition is very strong, and is directed toward something definite, every action of your mind, every action of your personality, and every action of your faculties will become constructive; that is, all those actions will be inspired by the tremendous force of your ambition to work for the realization of that ambition.

Never permit restless ambition. Whenever you feel the force of ambition, direct your mind at once in a calm, determined manner upon that which you really want to accomplish in life. Make this a daily practice, and you will steadily train all your faculties and powers not only to work for the realization of that ambition, but become more and more efficient in that direction. Before long your forces and faculties will be sufficiently competent to accomplish what you want.

In the proper use of the mind therefore, these three essentials should be applied constantly and thoroughly. First, direct all the powers of mind, all the powers of thought, and all your thinking upon the goal you have in view. Second, train every mental action to be deeply and calmly positive. Third, train every mental action to be constructive, to be filled with a building Spirit, to be inspired with a ceaseless desire to develop the greater, to achieve the greater, to attain the greater. When you have acquired these three, you will begin to use your forces in such a way that results must follow. You will begin to move forward steadily and surely, and you will be constantly gaining ground. Your mind will have become like the stream mentioned above.

It will gather volume and force as it moves on and on, until finally that volume will be great enough to remove any obstacle in its way, and that force powerful enough to do anything you may have in view.

In order to apply these three essentials in the most effective manner, there are several misuses of the mind that must be avoided. Avoid the forceful, the aggressive, and the domineering attitudes, and do not permit your mind to become intense, unless it is under perfect control. Never attempt to control or influence others in any way whatever. You will seldom succeed in that manner, and when you do, the success will be temporary; besides, such a practice always weakens your mind.

Do not turn the power of your mind upon others, but turn it upon yourself in such a way that it will make you stronger, more positive, more capable, and more efficient. As you develop in this manner, success must come of itself. There is only one way you can influence others legitimately and that is through the giving of instruction, but in that case, there is no desire to influence. You desire simply to impart knowledge and information, and you exercise a most desirable influence without desiring to do so.

A great many men and women, after discovering the immense power of mind, have come to the conclusion that they might change circumstances by exercising mental power upon those circumstances in some mysterious manner, but such a practice means nothing but a waste of energy.

The way to control circumstances is to control the forces within yourself to make a greater human being of yourself, and as you become greater and more competent, you will naturally gravitate into better circumstances. In this connection, we should remember that like attracts like. If you want that which is better, make yourself better. If you want to realize the ideal, make yourself more ideal. If you want better friends, make yourself a better friend. If you want to associate with people of worth, make yourself more worthy. If you want to meet that which is agreeable, make yourself more agreeable. If you want to enter conditions and circumstances that are more pleasing, make yourself more pleasing. In brief, whatever you want, produce that something in yourself, and you will positively gravitate towards the corresponding conditions in the external world.

But to improve yourself along those lines, it is necessary to apply for that purpose all the power you possess. You cannot afford to waste any of it, and every misuse of the mind will waste power. Avoid all destructive attitudes of the mind, such an anger, hatred, malice, envy, jealousy, revenge, depression, discouragement, disappointment, worry, fear, and so on. Never antagonize, never resist what is wrong, and never try to get even. Make the best use of your own talent and the best that is in store for you will positively come your way. When others seem to take advantage of you, do not retaliate by trying to take advantage of them. Use your power in improving yourself, so that you can do better and better work. That is how you are going to win in the race.

Later on, those who tried to take advantage of you will be left in the rear. Remember, those who are dealing unjustly with you or with anybody are misusing their mind. They are therefore losing their power, and will, in the course of time, begin to lose ground; but if you, in the mean time, are turning the full power of your mind to good account, you will not only gain more power, but you will soon begin to gain ground. You will gain and continue to gain in the long run, while others who have been misusing their minds will lose mostly everything in the long run. That is how you are going to win, and win splendidly regardless of ill treatment or opposition.

A great many people imagine that they can promote their own success by trying to prevent the success of other, but it is one of the greatest delusions in the world. If you want to promote your own success as thoroughly as your capacity will permit, take an active interest in the success of everybody, because this will not only keep your mind in the success attitude and cause you to think success all along the line, but it will enlarge your mind so as to give you a greater and better grasp upon the fields of success. If you are trying to prevent the success of others, you are acting in the destructive attitude, which sooner or later will react on others, but if you are taking an active interest in the success of everybody, you are entertaining only constructive attitudes, and these will sooner or later accumulate in your own mind to add volume and power to the forces of success that you are building up in yourself.

In this connection, we may well ask why those succeed who do succeed, why so many succeed only in part, and why so many fail utterly. These are questions that occupy the minds of most people, and hundreds of answers have been given, but there is only one answer that goes to rock bottom.

Those people who fail, and who continue to fail all along the line, fail because the power of their minds is either in a habitual negative state, or is always misdirected. If the power of mind is not working positively and constructively for a certain goal, you are not going to succeed. If your mind is not positive, it is negative, and negative minds float with the stream. We must remember that we are in the midst of all kinds of circumstances, some of which are for us and some of which are against us, and we will either have to make our own way or drift, and if we drift we go wherever the stream goes. But most of the streams of human life are found to float in the world of the ordinary and the inferior. Therefore, if you drift, you will drift with the inferior, and your goal will be failure.

When we analyze the minds of people who have failed, we invariably find that they are either negative, non-constructive or aimless. Their forces are scattered, and what is in them is seldom applied constructively. There is an emptiness about their personality that indicates negativity. There is an uncertainty in their facial expression that indicates the absence of definite ambition. There is nothing of a positive, determined nature going on in their mental world.

They have not taken definite action along any line. They are dependent upon fate and circumstances. They are drifting with some stream, and that they should accomplish little if anything is inevitable. This does not mean, however, that their mental world is necessarily unproductive; in fact, those very minds are in many instances immensely rich with possibilities. The trouble is, those possibilities continue to be dormant, and what is in them is not being brought forth and trained for definite action or actual results.

What these people should do is to proceed at once to comply with the three essentials mentioned above, and before many months there will be a turn in the lane. They will soon cease to drift, and will then begin to make their own life, their own circumstances, and their own future. In this connection, it is well to remember that negative people and non-constructive minds never attract that which is helpful in their circumstances. The more you drift, the more people you meet who also drift, while on the other hand, when you begin to make your own life and become positive, you begin to meet more positive people and more constructive circumstances. This explains why "God helps them that help themselves." When you begin to help yourself, which means to make the best of what is in yourself, you begin to attract to yourself more and more of those helpful things that may exist all about you. In other words, constructive forces attract constructive forces; positive forces attract positive forces. A growing mind attracts elements and forces that help to promote growth, and people who are determined to make more and more of themselves are drawn more and more into circumstances through which they will find the opportunity to make more of themselves. And this law works not only in connection with the external world, but also the internal world.

When you begin to make a positive determined use of those powers in yourself that are already in positive action, you draw forth into action powers within you that have been dormant, and as this process continues, you will find that you will accumulate volume, capacity, and power in your mental world until you finally become a mental giant. As you begin to grow and become more capable, you will find that you will meet better and better opportunities, not only opportunities for promoting external success, but opportunities for further building yourself up along the lines of ability, capacity, and talent.

You thus demonstrate the law that "Nothing succeeds like success," and "To him that hath shall be given." And here it is well to remember that it is not necessary to possess external things in the beginning to be counted among them "that hath." It is only necessary in the beginning to possess the interior riches; that is, to take control of what is in you, and proceed to use it positively with a definite goal in view. He who has control of his own mind has already great riches. He has sufficient wealth to be placed among those who have. He is already successful, and if he continues as he has begun, his success will soon appear in the external world. Thus the wealth that existed at first in the internal only will take shape and form in the external. This is a law that is unfailing, and there is not a man or woman on the face of the earth that cannot apply it with the most satisfying results.

The positive and constructive use of the power of mind with a definite goal in view will invariably result in advancement, attainment, and achievement. But if we wish to use that power in its full capacity, the action of the mind must be deep. In addition to the right use of the mind, we must also learn the full use of mind. This implies the use of the whole mind, the deeper mental fields and forces, as well as the usual mental fields and forces.[xxii]

*Revised and Edited from the works of Larson [xxiii]

The Science of Gratitude in Twenty-Five Parts . [xxiv]

1.   You believe that there is one intelligent substance from which all things proceed. Second, you believe that this substance gives you everything you desire. And third, you relate yourself to it by a feeling of deep and profound gratitude.

2.   The world is overflowing with good things, because life is in touch with the limitless source of all good things, and there is so much of everything that the wish of every heart can be gratified.

3.   We do not have to take from another to have abundance, because there is more than sufficient for all. The fact that some one has abundance does not prove that he has taken some or all of his wealth from others, although this is what a great many believe to be the truth

4.   Whenever we see someone in luxury we wonder where and how he got it, and we usually add that many are in poverty because this one is in wealth. Such a doctrine, however, is not true. It is thoroughly false from beginning to end. The world is not so poverty stricken that the few cannot have plenty without stealing from the many.

5.   God is rich; the Universe is overflowing with abundance. If we have not everything that we want, there is a reason; there is some definite cause somewhere, either in ourselves or in our relations to the world, but this cause can be found and corrected; then we may proceed to take possession of our own.

6.   Among the many causes of poverty and the lack of a full supply there is one that has been entirely overlooked. To overcome this cause is to find one of the most important paths to perpetual increase, and the remedy lies within easy reach of everyone who has awakened to a degree the finer elements in their life.

7.   There may be exceptions to the rule, but there are thousands who are living on the husks of existence because they were not grateful when the kernels were received. Multitudes continue in poverty from no other cause than a lack of gratitude, and other thousands who have almost everything that the heart may wish for do not reach the coveted goal of full supply *because their gratitude is not complete.*

8.   If it is a New Thought to you that gratitude brings your whole mind into closer harmony with the creative energies of the Universe, consider it well, and you will see that it is true. Having received one gift from God, they cut the wires that connect them with him by failing to make acknowledgment.

9.   The grateful outreaching of your mind in thankful praise to the supreme intelligence is a liberation or expenditure of force. It cannot fail to reach that to which it addressed, and the reaction is an instantaneous movement toward you.

10.   We are now beginning to realize more and more that the greatest thing in the world is to live so closely to the Infinite that we constantly feel the power and the peace of His presence. But the value of gratitude does not consist solely in getting you more

blessings in the future. Without gratitude you cannot long keep from dissatisfied thought regarding things as they are.

11.   In fact, this mode of living is the very secret of secrets revealing everything that the mind may wish to know or understand in order to make life what it is intended to be. We also realize that the more closely we live to the Infinite the more we shall receive of all good things, because all good things have their source in the Supreme; but how to enter into this life of supreme oneness with the Most High is a problem.

12.   There are many things to be done in order to solve this problem, but there is no one thing that is more important in producing the required solution than deep, whole-souled gratitude. The soul that is always grateful lives nearer the true, the good, the beautiful and the perfect than anyone else in existence, and the more closely we live to the good and the beautiful the more we shall receive of all those things. The mind that dwells constantly in the presence of true worth is daily adding to its own worth. It is gradually and steadily appropriating that worth with which it is in constant contact; but we cannot enter into the real presence of true worth unless we fully appreciate the real worth of true worth; and all appreciation is based upon gratitude.

13.   The grateful mind is constantly fixed upon the best. Therefore it tends to become the best. It takes the form or character of the best, and will receive the best. Also, faith is born of gratitude. The grateful mind continually expects good things, and expectation becomes faith.

The reaction of gratitude upon one's own mind produces faith, and every outgoing wave of grateful thanksgiving increases faith.

14.   Notice the grateful attitude that Jesus took, how he always seems to be saying, "I thank thee, Father, that thou hearest me." You cannot exercise much power without gratitude, for it is gratitude that keeps you connected with power.

15.   The more grateful we are for the good things that come to us now the more good things we shall receive in the future. This is a great metaphysical law, and we shall find it most profitable to comply exactly with this law, no matter what the circumstances may be. Be grateful for everything and you will constantly receive more of everything; thus the simple act of being grateful becomes a path to perpetual increase. The reason is that the mental attitude of real gratitude will draw you in much closer contact with that power that produces the good things received.

16.   In other words, to be grateful for what we have received is to draw more closely to the source of that which we receive. The good things that come to us come because we have properly employed certain laws, and when we are grateful for the results gained we enter into more perfect harmony with those laws and thus become able to employ those laws to still greater advantage in the immediate future. This anyone can understand, and those who do not know that gratitude produces this effect should try it and watch results.

17.   The attitude of gratitude brings the whole mind into more perfect and more harmonious relations with all the laws and powers of life. The grateful mind gains a firmer hold, so to speak, upon those things in life that can produce increase. This is simply illustrated in personal experience where we find that we always feel nearer to that person to whom we express real gratitude. When you thank a person and truly mean it with heart and soul you feel nearer to that person than you ever did before. Likewise, when we express whole-souled thanksgiving to everything and everybody for everything that comes into life we draw closer and closer to all the elements and powers of life.

18.   The moment you permit your mind to dwell with dissatisfaction upon things as they are, you begin to lose ground. You fix attention upon the common, the ordinary, the poor, the squalid, and the mean, and your mind takes away your power and you become distracted. The person who has no feeling of gratitude cannot long retain a living faith.

19.   In other words, we draw closer to the real source from which all good things in life proceed. When we consider this principle from another point of view we find that the act of being grateful is an absolute necessity, if we wish to accomplish as much as we have the power to accomplish. To be grateful in this large, universal sense is to enter into harmony and contact with the greatest, the highest, and the best in life. We thus gain possession of the superior elements of mind and soul, and, in consequence, gain the power to become more and achieve more, no matter what our object or work may be. Everything

that will place us in a more perfect relation with life, and thus enable us to appropriate the greater richness of life, should be employed with the greatest of earnestness, and deep whole- souled gratitude does possess a marvelous power in this respect. Its great value, however, is not confined to the laws just mentioned. Its power is exceptional in another and equally important field.

20.   To be grateful is to think of the best, therefore the grateful mind keeps the eye constantly upon the best; and, according to another metaphysical law, we grow into the likeness of that which we think of the most. The mind that is always dissatisfied fixes attention upon the common, the ordinary, and the inferior, and thus grows into the likeness of those things. The creative forces within us are constantly making us just like those things upon which we habitually concentrate attention. Therefore, to mentally dwell upon the inferior is to become inferior, while to keep the eye single upon the best is to daily become better. The grateful mind is constantly looking for the best, thus holding attention upon the best and daily growing into the likeness of the best. The grateful mind expects only good things, and will always secure good things out of everything that comes. What we constantly expect we receive, and when we constantly expect to get good out of everything we cause everything to produce good.

21.   Therefore, to the grateful mind all things will at all times work together for good, and this means perpetual increase in everything that can add to the happiness and the welfare of man. This being true, and anyone can prove it to be true, the proper course to pursue is to cultivate the habit of being grateful for everything that comes.

22.   Give thanks eternally to the Most High for everything and feel deeply grateful every moment to every living creature. All things are so situated that they can be of some service to us, and all things have somewhere at some time been instrumental in adding to our welfare.

23.   We must therefore, to be just and true, express perpetual gratitude to everything that has existence. Be thankful to yourself. Be thankful to every soul in the world, and most of all be thankful to the Creator of all that is. Live in perpetual thanksgiving to all the world, and express the deepest, sincerest, most whole-souled gratitude you can feel within whenever something of value comes into your life. When other things come, pass them by; never mind them in the least.

24.   You know that the good in greater and greater abundance is eternally coming into your life, and for this give thanks with rejoicing; you know that every wish of the heart is being supplied; be thankful that this is true, and you will draw nearer and nearer to that place in life where what can be realized that you know is on the way to realization. Live according to this principle for a brief period of time, and the result will be that your life will change for the better to such a degree that you will feel infinitely more grateful than you ever felt before.

25.   You will then find that thanksgiving and a grateful heart are necessary parts of real living, and you will also find that the more grateful you are for every ideal that has been made real, the more power you gain to press on to those greater heights where you will find every ideal to be real. And when this realization begins you are

on the path to perpetual increase, because the more you receive the more grateful you feel, and the more grateful you feel for that which has been received the more closely you will live to that Source that can give you more.

These twenty-five parts were compiled, prepared, and extracted from the teachings and publications of Wallace D. Wattles, Christian D. Larson, Thomas Troward, and Charles Haanel. These twenty-five elements of gratitude and abundance have been compiled and enhanced by Prof. Mentz. All of these authors published their philosophies that were used herein before 1920. * Please understand that anything that you praise, bless, thank, appreciate, or express gratitude towards, will be drawn to you. [xxv]

Beatitudes: A Brief Analysis & Positive Meanings [xxvi]

The Beatitudes (Latin: beatitudo, happiness) is the name given to the best-known & introductory portion of the Sermon on the Mount of the Gospel of

Matthew. For purposes of analyzing the mindset of abundance, we show each basic part of the Beatitudes and provide some insight into the highest meaning of each.

1.   **Poor in Spirit – Theirs is the Kingdom of Heaven -** This means that we should be teachable, be willing to grow. Humility is understanding your right size, putting the source of good first, and putting spirit before ego.

2.   **Mourn – They will be Comforted -** This implies that we should turn our will toward the Spirit. Understand your private emotions and transcend the instincts that may result in destructive thinking and action.

3.   **The Meek – Shall Inherit the Earth -** Forgive, clean house, receive forgiveness. Through self analysis, meditation, or focused prayer and visualization, you can allow for the highest thoughts to enter your spiritual mind.

4.   **Those who Hunger – They will be filled. -** Remain hungry for insight and guidance. Never give up. The mind is connected to ALL and is a benefactor of the greatest of wisdom if it is allowed to receive prosperous intelligence.

5.   **The Merciful – Will obtain Mercy -** Think and project love and gratitude. Radiate your good toward all including those who may have hurt you in the past. It is key for you to rise above past hurts and become the best you can be while also affording kind acts toward others that will help them grow.

6.   **The Pure in Heart – Will See God -** Our thinking, our actions and our omissions are part of our mind and character. Keeping a mind directed toward the highest good will always expand your abundance and flow of it toward you.

7.   **The Peacemakers – Will be the Children of God -** Bring Harmony, win-win relationships to all without facilitating injury toward yourself or to your family.

8.   The Persecuted – Theirs in the Kingdom of Heaven - Experience and feel: a catharsis, absolution, forgiveness, and wholeness. Keep in mind that the self can give the illusion of self persecution. Your duty is to transcend your lower mental states with peace, love, abundance, and gratitude. [xxvii]

12 Steps of Abundance and Right Thinking with Scripture Comparison Notes on the Right. xxviii

Step 1: Admitted that ego and self is limited, and that living under this power of self and destructive thinking has resulted in a life of frustration without peace of mind.	I know that nothing good lives in me, that is, in my sinful nature. For I have the desire to do what is good, but I cannot carry it out. (Romans 7:18)
Step 2: Came to believe that the personal recognition of Spiritual abundance within my own being and without would allow prosperity in my life.	Jesus said unto him, If thou canst believe, all things are possible to him that believeth. And straightway the father of the child cried out, and said with tears, Lord, I believe; help thou mine unbelief. (Mark 9:23-24)
Step 3: Made a decision to seek Spirit before ego by seeking a harmonious relationship with the Universal Spirit Force of abundance.	If anyone would come after me, he must deny himself and take up his cross daily and follow me. (Luke 9:23**)
Step 4: I engage in self-analysis for the purpose of removing wasteful thought energy.	Let us examine our ways and test them, and let us return to the Lord. (Lamentations 3:40)

Step 5: I expose to my higher self and another human being the exact nature of the destructive thoughts and actions of the past.	Therefore confess your sins to each other and pray for each other so that you may be healed. (James 5:16)
Step 6: I became willing to have the Universal Spirit remove my destructive beliefs in favor of building my own character of goodness and prosperity.	If you are willing and obedient, you will eat the best from the land. (Isaiah 1:19)
Step 7: I humbly asked the Universal Spirit to remove my consciousness of fear, failure, poverty, or inadequacy.	Humble yourselves before the Lord, and He will lift you up. (James 4:10)

Step 8: I made a list of all relationships gone bad and became willing to allow the Universal Spirit mend my soul and heart and allow *my* forgiveness permanently.	Therefore, if you are offering your gift at the altar and there remember that your brother has something against you, leave your gift there in front of the altar. First go and be reconciled to your brother; then come and offer your gift. (Matthew 5:23, 24**)
Step 9: I allow the Universal Spirit to help me heal relationships	Give and it shall be given you. A good measure, pressed down,

wherever possible, except when to do so would create more harm than good to all parties involved.	shaken together and running over, will be poured into your lap. For with the measure you use, it will be measured to you. (Luke 6:38**)
Step 10: I continue to periodically analyze my thinking, and immediately recognize and correct error consciousness while avoiding destructive actions.	For by the grace given me I say to every one of you: Do not think of yourself more highly than you ought, but rather think of yourself with sober judgment, in accordance with the measure of faith GOD has given you. (Romans 12:3)
Step 11: I Seek to maintain a harmonious, grateful and thankful relationship with my inner self and with The Universal Spirit of abundance.	Let the word of Christ dwell in you richly. (Col. 3:16)
Step 12: Having become Spiritually awake as a result of these steps, I carried this message to others, and practiced these principles in my life affairs.	Brothers, if someone is caught in a sin, you who are Spiritual should restore him gently. But watch yourself, or you also may be tempted. Carry each other's burdens, and in this way you will fulfill the law of Christ. (Galatians 6:1-2)

Special Exercises and Journal Writing

Here are some written exercises for growth and suggested questions for you to try to answer. Be proud of yourself for completing this book and attempting these exercises.

1.   If you could not fail, what would you do with your life in your work, financial life, or relationships?

2.   Write down as many accomplishments that you have been successful with. Begin with a diploma you received, a good job with family or work, or any job that you done.

3.   Write down who you think you are: Example: I am a good parent, I am of Irish decent, I am a Spiritual Person. Etc.

4.   Write down some ways in which you honor and respect yourself. Example: I go to the gym and eat right etc.

5.   Write down some ways that you may pamper yourself. Example: Long Bath, Read Books, Play Sports, Quality time with loved ones etc.

6.   Write down your 10 favorite types of labor that you enjoy that you consider fun. Example: Working with people, travel related jobs, creating things etc.

7.   Write down 10 things you could do that would dramatically improve you life. Keep this list open to addition and subtraction.

8.   Write down 10-20 attributes about yourself or things that you are thankful for. Keep this list open to addition.

9.   Write down 10 things that you like to do or would like to do to enjoy life more. Examples: Movies, Reading, Bowling, Travel

10.   Take out your resume and update it. Don't be shy and add to your resume anything that you have done for yourself, the community, your job, or any skills that you may have learned.

11.   Write out a list of your creative ideas. What would you like to start, build, create, or solve.

12.   Who are your favorite authors? Why? Did they inspire you?

13.   Write out an appreciation list? Name the people who have helped you in your life? Honor them with a blessing.

14.   Write out things you like about yourself and your best qualities.

15.   What can you do to become a better listener and hear what others are saying to us.

16.   What can you do to obtain greater peace of mind? How can we limit resentments, anger, and conflict while also protecting ourselves from any attack or abuse?

17.   What can you do to become better prepared for life, success, financial challenges, educational or skills advancement, and self respect?

18.   How can we learn better to communicate with others and also discuss our dreams and plans?

19.   What can you/I do to better care for my body and mental health.

20.   How can we be more attractive, more loving, more compassionate, & more helpful without doing more harm than good.

21.   What calculated risks do you fear that would really benefit you and maybe your family. Example: Going back to school.

22.   What can you do to better develop a harmonious relationship with yourself, your own ego, your higher self, the universe or GOD.

23.   What can we do to better cultivate a thankful heart and a mind of more constructive thoughts.

24.   What can we do to further develop our character and integrity.

25.   If you could live or travel anywhere in the world, where would it be? Why? What would you do there?

26.   Is there anyone in the world who really deserves an apology from you? Why? Would it help? Ask your spiritual counselor before taking this step any further.

27.   Is there anyone in the world that you still hate? Could you pray for them once a day for 30 days? Why or Why Not? If this guaranteed relief, would you be willing to try.

28.   Are you willing to honestly discuss your faults, strengths, and hopes with another person? Why? Or Why Not? If this would help you grow into a better person, can you try?

29.   Are you willing to give more than is required in service, value, and quality?

30.   Are you willing to keep a written list of several things to do each day toward your dreams? Can you try to do a few things effectively each day toward your ideals? [xxix]

An Exercise – Visualization for Manifesting

1. In a quiet spot, enter your relaxed state of mind and take a few deep breaths.
2. Relax each part of the body - one by one.
3. Close your eyes and imagine a snapshot picture of something that you really want to happen in your life.
4. Detail the final result of this wish using colors and 5 senses.
5. Imagine the emotions that you would have when this dream or goal or result is reached. FEEL the emotions of joy and thankfulness.
6. Harvest the mental essence of how having the result or thing will function in your life, serve you, and help all involved.
7. Believe that it has happened in your mind and allow yourself to imagine the ownership of this result mentally.
8. Pinpoint and focus on the completed final event of success. i.e. The foot race is completed OR the check is in your bank account.
9. Experience love and grateful feelings when you recognize and realize your vision. Know and Feel it "AS IF" it is FACT.
10. Imagine the benefits for all involved.
11. Be willing to receive all of this good on a mental and spiritual level which allows you to take actions toward creation and receiving the results
12. Make sure you have created ways to capture the result. Example: You may not be able to become the highest paid pilot without a license.

13.   Send this mental vision into the world with joy as a "thought centered" letter to the supreme architect.

14.   Respond to communication from others and your messages of intuition that come to you. Be willing to meet others half way and go the extra mile.

15.   Allow your dreams to unfold on parallel lines. Example: You may want a successful business in selling this one thing, but the laws of attraction may allow you to sell many other things related to it.

Thoughts on Scripture – Classic Laws of New Thought

To many, Scripture may not come to mind with daily challenges. However, once we have reflected on the ancient and proven teachings of these Transformational Teachings, we see that the keys to having an effective spiritual life are available for our growth.

1. We I think of lack or limitation, I now think of the Teachings of "**Laws of Abundance**" John 10:10 "The thief comes only to steal and kill and destroy; I have come that they might have life, and that they might have it more abundantly.

2. When I worry about my perception and the truth, I can reflect on the "**Law of Thought**" Matthew 6:22 "The **eye** is the **lamp** of the body. If your **eye**s are good, your whole body will be full of light.

3. When I want to procrastinate, I can remember the "**Law of Action**" and take steps each day toward improving my body, mind and spirit. Luke 9:62 Jesus replied, "No one who puts his hand to the plow and looks back is fit for service in the kingdom of God."

4. When I have annoying thoughts, I can consider the "**Law of Love**" Matthew 22: 36 Jesus replied: " 'Love the Lord your God with all your heart and with all your soul and with all your mind.'[b] 38This is the

first and greatest commandment. 39 And the second is like it: 'Love your neighbor as yourself.'[c] 40 All the Law and the Prophets hang on these two commandments."

5. When I wonder about my capabilities and ability to serve, The "**Law of Success**" must be pondered. John 14:12 "The works that I do shall he do also; and greater works than these shall he do."

6. When I want to react or become overly attached to a situation instead of being still, walking away, or responding in spiritual manner, the " **Law of Non Resistance**" comes to mind. Matthew 5:39 *Resist not Evil….*

7. When I wonder about the government and authority, I recall the "Law of Obedience" Mark 12:17 "Give to Caesar what is Caesar's, and to God what is God's." I then realize that my spiritual life transcends over politics.

8. When I am harboring anger or resentment, I try to observe the "Law of Forgiveness" and the freedom that I receive by giving forgiveness, praying for others, and allowing myself to be forgiven. Luke 6:37 [*Judging Others*] "Do not judge, and you will not be judged. Do not

condemn, and you will not be condemned. **Forgive**, and you will be **forgive**n.

9. When I wonder if things will improve, I must give credence to the "Law of Increase" and to consider helping others and serving humanity. Luke 6:38 Give, and it will be given to you. A good measure, pressed down, shaken together and running over, will be poured into your lap. For with the measure you use, it will be measured to you."

10.   When I feel unworthy, I should observe the "**Law of Receiving**" and become open to receiving and having a blessed life. Luke 16:12 "And if you have not been trustworthy with someone else's property, who will give you property of your own?"

11.   When I feel lazy or unmotivated, the "**Law of Compensation**" often comes to mind and I try a little harder to plant good seeds of work into the world. Galatians 6:7 "For whatsoever a man soweth, that shall he also **reap**.

12.	When I don't feel like preparing or becoming ready to embrace life, I sometimes consider the "Law of Preparedness" <u>Matthew 22:14</u> "For many are called, but few *are* chosen."

13.	When I lose focus on the good and become distracted from my purpose, the "**Laws of Attraction**" are indeed worth respecting. <u>Matthew 6:21</u> For where your treasure is, there your heart will be also

14.	When I am afraid to take risks, ask for help, change or grow, the "**Law of Supply**" is sometimes the secret to my transformation. <u>Matthew 7:7</u> [*Ask, Seek, Knock*] "**Ask** and it will be given to you; seek and you will find; knock and the door will be opened to you.

Affirmations

A Classic Abundant Health Treatment Exercise and Meditation

Take a time when you can have from twenty minutes to half an hour secure from interruption, and proceed first to make yourself physically comfortable. Lie at ease in a chair, or on a couch, or in bed; it is best to lie flat on your back. If you have no other time, take the exercise on going to bed at night and before rising in the morning.

First let your attention travel over your body from the crown of your head to the soles of your feet, relaxing every muscle as you go. Relax completely. And next, get physical and other ills off your mind. Let the attention pass down the spinal cord and out over the nerves to the extremities, and as you do so think: "My nerves are in perfect order all over my body. They obey my will, and I have great nerve force." Next bring your attention to the lungs and think: "I am breathing deeply and quietly, and the air goes into every cell of my lungs, which are in perfect condition. My blood is purified and made clean." Next, to the heart: "My heart is beating strongly and steadily, and my circulation is perfect, even to the extremities."

Next, to the digestive system: "My stomach and intestines perform their work perfectly. My food is digested and assimilated and my body rebuilt and nourished. My liver, kidneys, and bladder each perform their several functions without pain or strain; I am perfectly well. My body is resting, my mind is quiet, and my soul is at peace."

Next: "I have no anxiety about financial or other matters. God, who is within me, is also in all things I want, impelling them toward me; all that I want is already given to me. I have no anxiety about my health, for I am perfectly well. I have no worry or fear whatever. "I rise above all temptation to moral evil. I cast out all greed, selfishness, and narrow personal ambition; I do not hold envy, malice, or enmity toward any living soul. I will follow no course of action which is not in accord 'with my highest ideals. I am right and I will do right.'"

Viewpoint

All is right with the world. It is perfect and advancing to completion. I will contemplate the facts of social, political, and industrial life only from this high viewpoint. Behold, it is all very good. I will see all human beings, all my acquaintances, friends, neighbors, and the members of my own household in the same way. They are all good. Nothing is wrong with the Universe; nothing can be wrong but my own personal attitude, and henceforth I keep that right. My whole trust is in God.

Consecration

I will obey my soul and be true to that within me that is highest. I will search within for the pure idea of right in all things, and when I find it I will express it in my outward life. I will abandon everything I have outgrown for the best I can think. I will have the highest thoughts concerning all my relationships, and my manner and action shall express these thoughts. I surrender my body to be ruled by my mind; I yield my mind to the dominion of my soul, and I give my soul to the guidance of God.

Identification and Reconciliation

There is but one substance and source, and of that I am made and with it I am one. It is my Father; I proceeded forth and came from it. My Father and I are one, and my Father is greater than I, and I do His will. I surrender myself to conscious unity with Pure Spirit; there is but one and that one is everywhere. I am one with the Eternal Consciousness.

Idealization

Form a mental picture of yourself as you want to be, and at the greatest height your imagination can picture. Dwell upon this for some little time, holding the thought: "This is what I really am; it is a picture of my own perfection and advancing to completion. I will contemplate the facts of social, political, and industrial life only from this high viewpoint. Behold, it is all very good. I will see all human beings, all my acquaintances, friends, neighbors, and the members of my own household in the same way. They are all good. Nothing is wrong with the Universe, nothing can he wrong but my own personal attitude, and henceforth I keep that right. My whole trust is in God.

Realization

I appropriate to myself the power to become what I want to be, and to do what I want to do. I exercise creative energy; all the power there is, is mine. I will arise and go forth with power and perfect confidence; I will do mighty works in the strength of the Lord, my God. I will trust and not fear, for God is with me. [xxx]

- Remember that simple pains and discomforts are sometimes signals to take action to better your physical health; however, many pains are the body at work healing and regenerating itself on a cellular and molecular level.

- As a note, you may be able to work this positive person in your MIND for other people.

Other Affirmations

Prosperity

I am the essence of success. The universe is full of creation and expands every day. New opportunities and new ideas flow to me. I open my heart to that power and participate in the divine ideas that come to me every minute of the day. I allow peace and prosperity in my heart, mind, and soul. I know that I am blessed, and I am thankful for the gift of creation and life expression.

Health

My body is a temple of creation; every organ in my body is nourished and revitalized each day. In time, my whole physical being is regenerated cell by cell. My mental ideal of myself is perfect. Because I am an offspring of perfect creation, I am made uniquely wonderful through this authority. My body is a vessel of my spirit and soul, which allows me to exist and create in this world. I respect my body and accept the power and opportunity of life, living and wholeness.

Attitude

My inner spiritual condition allows me to have a high viewpoint of the world. I see the world as a place of kindness, and I become open to receiving the blessings of goodness from others. I see the best in others and myself. I am worthy of success and a wonderful life.

Love

I do all I can to maintain a consciousness of love in my mind. I forgive all those who have passed through my life. I want the best for everyone and hope that all can live in harmony, peace, love, and abundance. I meditate on the words of compassion, understanding, peace, humility, kindness, generosity, and selflessness.

Gratitude

I am grateful to all those who have come before me. I am thankful to the supreme creative power for life, peace, health, and the ability to love. Gratitude and a thankful heart keep me connected to power. Gratitude allows me to have faith and the knowledge that I can exist in a higher order of being.

Success

I am successful. I am worthy of prosperity, abundance, health, and happiness. Each day my life becomes better and better.

Poetic Prayers for Protection, Love, Forgiveness and Health

Protection Prayer – Recite 3X
Father's Love, Forever Bright
Divine Mothers' Emerging Light
Surround My Soul With your Affection
Your Super Power Gives Me/Us Protection

Love Prayer – Recite 3X
Mighty Peace is in My Heart
Where Love Prevails, a Magic Art
I Close My Eyes, I am Made Whole
As God's True Love Engulfs My Soul
In My Mind & Three Times Three
I Feel All Love AND Unity.

Forgiveness Prayer – Recite 3X
Purity is My Divine Right
The Force of Calm is in My Sight
The Power of Healing Light Within
Free Forever of Any Sin
I Clear Away All Old Debris
Where Now I Master Destiny.

Health 3X Prayer
My Every Cell in Harmony
My Body Whole Perfect & Free
As Love Lives Strong With ALL Above
My Heart Transcends to Master Love
Where Body and Soul Are Healed & Whole
The Supreme Force Renews My Soul.

New Thought - Metaphysical Issues & Insights

Harmonious Relationships:

Connected with all there is that is good, harvesting and having a harmonious relationship with the world through various philosophical exercises, using gratitude for any of your gifts on a daily basis can grow your expectation of good and faith. It is much easier to be connected when you have set aside or removed destructive thinking such as resentments, jealously or the seven deadly sins.

Desires

Desires are good and excellent. Desires can focus you on enriching your life and following your true direction. Cultivating desires into reality is vital for change, innovation, and improvement. You would not have a desire unless it was possible, but select desires where you have a solid sphere of possibility. An earnest and heartfelt desire is what allows us to seize upon opportunities and develop plans.

Plans

A plan or objective is fundamental in the clarification and specificity of your desire. A large majority of people are afraid to specify what they intend to do. Transcending this fear and taking bold action upon your plans and strategies allows for the growth and manifestation of your idea into a reality

Vision

A vision is important in that you clarify the path to your short-term and long-term enrichment of yourself, your goals, teamwork, or relationships.

Mission

A mission is important in that you can quantify and clarify a path to an outcome or ending strategy.

Having, Emotion, and Feelings

Mentally understanding the outcome or result as if you have it already is very important. It also allows you to qualify the consequences. It further provides you with feelings surrounding the outcome. Harvesting positive feelings surrounding the outcome is very important to energize a desire, mission, visualization, and result.

Visualization, Pictures, Imagination, Sending It Out

Mental visualization of your objectives holds great importance in the clarity of what you intend to do along the way and what you desire as an end result. Seeing what you intend to do and what you desire and plan as if it is real is a complex mental exercise, but vital to the codification and building of the objective so as to assist the manifestation of the result. Seeing *exactly* what you desire and intend causes you to specify your wants and desires. The stronger and longer you can hold your ideal in your mind's eye, the better.

Attention Focus

Pointing your mental faculties toward the individual actions required to achieve a task, project, or goal is what causes effectiveness, as long as your acts are efficient. Continuous and persistent thinking and action toward your work, goal, project, or desired outcome can funnel or intensify the energy in a specific direction.

Efficiently and Effectively

Completion and closure of acts and tasks one-by-one in a successful manner is what creates momentum toward an objective with no need to go backward.

Presence, Awareness, Doing

Thinking and planning are most crucial. However, boldness and action are what may cause events to happen and people to be attracted to you. Therefore, contemplation mixed with action is the optimal, blended solution.

Cause/Effect: "Like Attracts Like"

Every action has a reaction. Types of actions and thoughts attract similar actions and thoughts. Kindness tends to bring kindness. Respect tends to bring respect. Additionally, constructive thinking tends to bring constructive opportunities and events to the individual.

Increase

All mankind tends to be attracted to those who can bring them more life or enrichment. If an individual projects life and opportunity, then he or she will attract similar minds.

Insight and Restraint

Insight and restraint contain the ability to think something over, discuss it with others, or seek out counsel from others who understand or know the subject well without acting hastily. Thus, the opinion of experts and consequences are a valid consideration in thinking and acting.

Love, Forgiveness, Harmony, Dissipating Discouragement

Cultivating love and forgiveness can dispel otherwise destructive thoughts. Great minds can look back on things they love or loved, and re-harness that emotion.

Minding Your Own Business

There is something very real in taking care of yourself and your affairs. As such, your enhanced mind, body, soul, and financial affairs allow you to help those whom you love and serve humanity in better ways. The best way to be of service to humanity and your loved ones is to make the best of yourself. It is called Self Respect./Love.

Gratitude, Enthusiasm, Faith

A sincere heartfelt gratitude for life and its gifts will allow the flow of good to you. Systematic recognition of people or things to be thankful for along with gratitude may facilitate an expectation of good and growth of inherent faith.

Integrating this confident expectation with your aspirations creates great power.

Guarded Speech, Response/Ability

Speaking of only positive things can attract opportunity and friends. Keeping your desires and goals close to you will keep them from becoming dissipated energy. Sharing your desires and goals with those who support, encourage, and assist you can be a positive exercise and help harvest constructive feedback.

Change/Insanity

Not evolving while continuing to do things that are failures or destructive actions tends to prevent any growth.

Creating Versus Competing

It seems that many people feel that competition causes a limited supply. However, from a supply or abundance standpoint, individuals can create without competing, to serve humanity. As an example, an individual who creates a new cure to solve a common health problem is not competing against the world, but helping it.

Right Livelihood and Labor of Love

Having a labor of love can cause effectiveness and efficiency through energetic work. Doing something that you believe in or selling a product that you have faith in, can make your job much easier or even fun. Having fun with work is a divine right.

Blessing, Praise, Protection, and Expansion

Persons who engage in a metaphysical approach seem to enjoy a greater state of well-being and success when they bless their relationship with the Universe, bless their loved ones, bless their home, and give thanks for their health on a daily basis.

Gratitude, Religion and Great Thinkers

If the only prayer you say in your life is "Thank you," that would suffice. -- **Meister Eckhart**

Take full account of the excellencies which you possess, and in gratitude remember how you would hanker after them, if you had them not. -- **Marcus Aurelius**

Judaism

In the Jewish faith, gratitude is a critical component of worship. In the Hebrew Scriptures, the Psalms are saturated with thanksgiving to God: "O Lord my God, I will give thanks to you forever" (30:12), and "I will give thanks to the Lord with my whole heart "(9:1).

Christianity

In the Christian faith, Philippians IV sums up the Christian attitude toward gratitude. See Below:

Philippians IV

4 Rejoice in the Lord always. Again I will say, rejoice!   5 Let your gentleness be known to all men. The Lord [is] at hand.   6 Be anxious for nothing, but in everything by prayer and supplication, with thanksgiving, let your requests be made known to God;   7 and the peace of God, which surpasses all understanding, will guard your hearts and minds through Christ Jesus.   8 Finally, brethren, whatever things are true, whatever things [are] noble, whatever things [are] just, whatever things [are] pure, whatever things [are] lovely, whatever things [are] of good report, if [there is] any virtue and if [there is] anything praiseworthy -- meditate on these things.   9 The things which you learned and received and heard and saw in me, these do, and the God of peace will be with you.   10 But I rejoiced in the Lord greatly that now at last your care for me has flourished again; though you surely did care, but you lacked opportunity.   11 Not that I speak in regard to need, for I have learned in whatever state I am, to be content: 12 I know how to be abased, and I know how to abound. Everywhere and in all things I have learned both to be full and to be hungry, both to abound and to suffer need.   13 I can do all things through Christ who strengthens me.

Read the above statements and passages from the Old Scriptures and other quotes and think about: gentleness, thanksgiving, constructive petitions, request for blessings, a sincere feeling of gratitude, meditating on noble and optimistic thoughts, rejoicing in life, and even blessing yourself and your future.

Unfolding Detachment Protected for Higher Good

When we become too attached or dependent on an external person, place, thing, or result, we can become disappointed with other people and things. It is good to expect the best, but it is also smart to allow for something better to unfold. Thus, trying to control a specific outcome without any flexibility can inhibit the Universe from its creativity.

Receiving, Valuing, Deserving

Many people from around the world feel unworthy of abundance. Many people do not value themselves, their service, their talents, and work. It is very important to learn to feel worthy, unique, and deserving of good. Moreover, you should become mentally open to receiving all good in life. Further, people should be careful to create ways to receive the good into their lives from the Universe and from others. Example: Accepting a compliment from another person.

Other People and When They Are Sent to Help You

When you engage a mentality of abundance and harmonious Spiritual thinking, your mind will expand and increase while radiating love, abundance, and health. Thus, your powers of attraction will increase. The Universe will send people to help you. It will be your job to select and allow them to assist you in a win-win relationship to expand your abundance where all can achieve a richer and fuller life through these joint ventures.

Resistance and Flow

Types of resistance that inhibit your abundance, health, and connection with Spirit are: resentment, jealousy, anger, judgment, criticism, hatred, greed, pride, and mental laziness. Other subtle resistance is to institutions, conformity, and adapting. It is better to adapt than to perish, while maintaining your unique qualities

Willingness

Willingness is the key to advancement. Be willing to take action, take a chance, or risk failure or embarrassment. Without willingness, you may never engage mental, Spiritual, or physical action that leads to good. Willingness is a vital ingredient toward successful visualization, belief, action, planning, and success. Am I willing to believe, to try, to risk, to engage? Can it be done? And why not?

Hoarding and Change

Holding onto old ideas, old things, and old ways can keep you from growth, Spiritual flow, and expansion. Taking an inventory of mental ideas and material things must be done. Eliminating the ideas, things, people, and actions that create inconvenience, frustration, clutter, and resentment will allow freedom and harmony in your life.

Recognition of Cause

It can be a fundamental mistake if you give yourself too much credit for anything good that you receive from life. Additionally, it can be a disastrous mistake to continue to blame God and the Universe for anything bad that you receive from life.

Sanity, Root Out Cause, Unlimited Potential

Root out the cause of your failures, your inconveniences, your frustration, and your mental or Spiritual disabilities. If you have a problem, there may be a cause. If you injured yourself engaging in a specific activity, you may avoid this activity in the future or better prepare for it next time. Otherwise, you may pay for this repeated action in the form of more pain and suffering. If you have a relationship that always seems to leave you in pain, then you may need to avoid this person if you are spiritually whole and the other person is not.

Giving Without Expectation, Tithing

Taking time to give money, service, or goods to divine recipients will create an untold flow in your life. Life requires circulation of your ideas, your things, and your service to humanity. With this giving, it is virtually guaranteed that your life will be blessed and protected through your giving of yourself. You are not doing this to take advantage of the law. You do this to expand your Spiritual existence, keep the flow, and give back. Expecting something in return is not needed because the Universe will provide opportunity for you by your embracing this process.

Wasting Energy and Thought

If you become frustrated every time you watch the news or read the newspaper, then why would you continue to read a specific article or watch that particular channel? It is vitally important for you to engage relaxing or strengthening activities rather than getting the same shot of bad medicine each day.

Good Deeds and Action / Balance Karma

You may feel you have wronged many people. You may even feel guilty for past deeds or encounters. However, if you feel remorse and intend to act as a better person for now on, then you have made progress. In any event, your day-to-day action and character of goodness and kindness will build your positive energy where the world has decided to protect you and serve you.

Meek Defined: Open Mind, Faith in Universe, Will of God, Spirit Before Ego

Meek is not weak. It is strong, confident, cooperative, and advantageous. Developing an honest appraisal of yourself can be healthy. You can always improve yourself, your credentials, your relationships and your business. Putting your ego first can be dangerous. When somebody has hurt your feelings, said you are wrong, said "no" to you, or otherwise attacked you, it is best to analyze (when possible) and discuss the issue with another supportive person before retaliating with e-mail, phone, letter, or in person.

Peace and Serenity Are Needed for Concentration

Peace allows growth. Clarity and concentration are primary keys to serenity. Being able to operate on a plane with singleness of mind can allow you to achieve great things. A person who cannot focus and achieve one thing at a time may never cross "the finish line" with any dream, goal, or aspiration. Overall, if you allow resentment, frustration, hate of another, or fear to dominate your thoughts, then your effectiveness will be diminished. Hard work is required to keep you focused and concentrating on bettering yourself. Overall, your freedom, vitality and wholeness depend on your effectiveness.

Visualizing Completed Transaction With Joy

We have mentioned visualization. Do not forget that you should visualize things and plans as you would have them. You should believe that they are yours in mind. Paint your ideal outcome on the mental screen in your mind's eye. Believe that it is completed. Fuse your image with love and gratitude. Celebrate its reception in your mind. Believe that you have the proper channels to receive what is coming to you. Send your vision and petition into the Universe and repeat the exercise for fantastic results.

Treasure Map and Wheel of Fortune

If you cannot paint the mental picture as clearly as you would want, then try to use the material world to enhance your mind. Cut out pictures of the ideal things you want. Put them into a collage or on poster board. Rip out images of the home you desire, people having fun, distant places that you want to visit, or the lifestyle and types of relationships that you desire. This action can help you amalgamate the images to imprint them on your subconscious mind. View them daily and place them in a prominent place. Overall, imagine having these things in your quite time. Sense the joy of receiving all of it fully.

Attraction by Thoughts

As for attraction, this can be of mind, action, and omission. You can think of something all day and possibly attract this. Further, you may act a certain way and either become it or attract it in your life. Moreover, your omissions of conduct may prevent you from steering into the direction of your life dreams.

When you consider your close family relationships, you may want to reevaluate how you respond to family members' mistakes, ideas, and thoughts. If you respond in a dubious fashion, your family members may not want to tell you about themselves. If your conversations are always woeful and negative, then your family members may consider you a toxic person. As such, if you are predisposed to being negative and a contrarian, you would probably attract others who seek to discuss the same theme with you or even try to better you in the experience of misery and misfortune. Also, your omissions are important also. If you refuse to help anyone, you may not be helped when you need it. If you omit tolerance and love to others, you may not receive it either. Thus, there is a delicate balance of give and take in the world. It is better to give now and then you shall be given to and provided for as time goes on.

With all of this in mind, it is far more practical to look at the possibilities of success, good ideas, magic, miracles, and more in others. See the God and genius in all of those you love and around you, and maybe it will be revealed and vitalized to and within you.

Exercises for Concentration, Meditation, and Energy

Concentration Exercise
1. Find a relaxed part of your home
2. Sit and quiet the mind and begin to relax each part of the body (that you can think of) from head to toes.
3. Shut your eyes & take a few deep breaths.
4. Think of a room that you lived in as a child or that you are presently in.
5. Begin to see and visualized in your mind the entire room and its contents and where things are located. (Whatever you can recall)
6. It is also good to imagine the exact color of things in the room with your eyes closed.
7. This is also a good exercise to do even after you have entered a new building or place.
8. Do this for a few minutes each day and your focus and concentration will increase. These days, there is computer software that actually runs programs to help concentration in this same way..
9. As a note, this same type of exercise is also very good to relax and vividly recall wonderful people or possessions that you have in your past or present.
- Open your eyes when done with any of these exercises ☺

Active Meditation Exercise
1. Engage steps 1, 2 & 3 above.
2. With eyes closed and imagining, see yourself going into a sacred castle.
3. As you enter the main chamber, you see the (helpful person of your choice).
4. This person could be alive or from the past.
5. You then discuss with her or him in your minds eye. [imagination]
6. You ask questions and your Friendly Guru answers these questions.
7. Try and sense the answers from your core (heart and stomach).
8. When you are finished, thank your friend for the help and guidance.
9. You may have an overwhelming sense that this voice or person is from a higher or different viewpoint than your own.

Exercise for Energizing or Healing Yourself.

1) Engage steps 1,2, and 3 above. (Relaxing in a chair with spine straight) relax your hands on your lap.
2) Close your eyes and visualize a peaceful lake that has no ripples. Then see yourself surrounded by bright white particles of energy that also permeates your body.
3) In your mind, see the bright light move toward and focus on the area of discomfort or pain. Allow this white light to fill any affected area and flow thought your body.
4) Know that the white light brings all of your body's healing power to work most effectively for you.
5) Take a few breaths.
6) Then, allow this bright light to act like water and flow though your body.
7) Allow the "fluid of light" purify and wash your entire body.
8) Feel and see in your minds eye that the washing fluid of white light is "pure love" and cleanses you of ANY AND ALL fear, resentment, hurt, and dis-ease.
9) Say to yourself, I forgive myself and everyone for the past. Thank the light of the universe for removing any impurities from your body.

10) Claim mental freedom from all problems in your mind and spirit. Thank the universe for your health and peace.
11) See others in your mind's eye walking up to you and congratulating you on your healing and success.
12) That's it….. & Open your eyes.

Perception and Awareness Exercise

1. Sit is a relaxed position
2. Relax each part of the body and take a few deep breaths.
3. Imagine a warm energy radiating through your body.
4. Enter what we call the Alpha State – which is Relaxed Daydreaming and Right Brain.
5. Now, begin to feel or sense each part of the body.
6. Direct your attention to your toes or hands or ears.
7. Notice how each part of the body feels.
8. Now close your eyes and notice any sounds either of your body or around you.
9. See if you can hear something far away.
10. Now, refocus and imagine just one sound or image.
11. Focus all of your thought on seeing, hearing, feeling, or tasting/smelling only one thing that you imagine.
12. Imagine this one thing to the exclusion of everything else.
13. As an example, try to imagine just the sound of a soft trumpet or French horn playing a song.
14. After a few minutes, relax again and come back to your BETA state of mind and consciousness. Left Brain

Affirmation Exercises

1. Affirmations should be affirmative. Each affirmation can be written in an "AS IF" phrase or sentence.
2. Affirmations can be for health, success, peace, safety, relationships, or even supply in the form of money.
3. Affirmations can be said out loud or in silence. Some people love to do their affirmations in the mirror.
4. A prime example of an affirmation could be, " I am healthy, happy, successfully, loved and whole. I am part Supreme Intelligence and the Supreme only creates beauty and perfection."
5. Keep in mind, you should have an "essence in back of affirmations". As an example, a supply affirmation could say, "I will earn an extra 5000 dollars in the next 4 weeks by providing excellent service as a salesperson or expert or by effectively serving others...."
6. As you can see, the above affirmation specifies some distinct creative work and cooperation related to your prosperity, and it is not a blind or hopeful demand to receive something for nothing. You can always affirm mentally or out loud for possibilities and opportunities.
7. There are primary reasons against blind affirmations for things or money of which we will not discuss at length. However, if a person demands 100 thousand dollars from the supreme, it may come in the form of an injury settlement which might not be your first choice.
8. Overall, we should state our affirmations with confidence, love, harmony, gratitude, and faith. With this combination, the universe will gladly begin working to unfold opportunities and blessings for you.
9. As such, a clear thought or idea that is repeated again and again is almost certain to manifest a replica of itself in the future. If the thought is held strongly, with gratitude and feeling, and in a creative way that does not hurt others, your desire will come quickly as the imagined formulation or something even better will unfold.

A BOLD New Thought Prayer for Peace –
– Edited and Composed By Sgr. G S Mentz - JD MBA

Lord, Let us be a Beacon of Light and Harmony. May we serve you to maximize the joy, health, abundance, and aliveness in and of our world.

- Where there is Struggle, may there be Freedom
- Where there is Hope, may there be Success
- Where there is Dis-Ease, may there be Wholeness and Healing.
- Where there is Peace, may there be Prosperity, Order, and Tranquility.
- Where there is Change, may there be Innovation.
- Where there is Love, may there be Respect, Honor and Civility.
- Where there is Mindfulness, may there be Illumination and Awakening.
- Where there is Consciousness, may there be Spirituality and Serenity.
- Where there is Confusion, may there be Knowingness and Belief.
- Where there is Wanting, may there by Actualization.
- Where there is Victimhood, may there be Victory.
- Where there is Atonement, may there be Attunement
- Where there is Decision, may there be ACTION and Commitment.
- Where there is Justice, may there be Inner-Peace.
- Where there is Poverty, may there be a Righteous Labor of Love.
- Where there is the Past, may we contribute to the NOW.
- Where there is Uncertainty, may there be Authentic Faith.
- Where there is Meditation, may there by Clarity.
- Where there is Intelligence, may there be Pure Awareness.
- Where there is Pain, may there be Growth.
- Where there is Emptiness, may we be Filled with Joy and Abundance.
- Where there is Unity, may there be Serenity.

Where there is Action, may we engage in Deeds that Stimulate Positive Outcomes. O' Great Master, let us seek to empathize rather than console, to comprehend rather than understand, to love rather than be loved. While it is in earnestly giving that one receives, it is by forgiving that we own our freedom, and it is in illumination that one finds. For it is in transformation that one transcends, and it is in rebirth that one is raised to eternal bliss.

When we are Contemplative in Action, We can Express our Destiny, and We will never Be Defeated if we have Elevated our Spirit and Mastered our Consciousness.

<u>*Here is a basic timetable of Esoteric Spirituality and Gnosticism*</u>

1. Zarathustra 1000-1500 BC Persia
2. Heraclitus – 6th Century BC
3. Pythagoras – Born 571 BC Century BC Greece – Italy
4. Laozi – Lao Tzu – Taoism Born 571 BC
5. Confucius Born 551 BC
6. Siddhartha Gautama (Buddhism) – 6th Century BC India
7. Socrates, Plato, Aristotle - 4th Century BC
8. Epicurus – 3rd Century BC
9. Cicero 40 BC
10.   Marcus Aurelius 180 AD
11.   Iamblichus 300 AD
12.   St. Benedict 5th Century
13.   Scottus Johannes Erigena – 9th Century
14.   Hildegard von Bingen – 11th Century
15.   Meister Eckhart 13th Century Mystic
16.   Hus – Jacob Boheme – Moravian Piety
17.   Rosicrucians – 14th Century
18.   Martin Luther – 16th Century
19.   Baruch Spinoza - 1632 – 1677
20.   von Zinzendorf und Pottendorf
21.   Liebniz 1710
22.   Hegel 1807
23.   Schopenhauer 1818
24.   Emerson and Thoreau 1860s – American Transcendentalism

25.	Theosophical Groups 1875 to present.

26.	Judge Thomas Troward 1900

27.	Carl Jung – Gnostic Mysticism

28.	Dr. Samuel M Shoemaker – Oxford Movement 1900-1940s

29.	Heȟáka Sápa, commonly known as Black Elk 1863-1950

30.	12 Step Programs – 1930s

31.	Dr. Norman Vincent Peale

32.	Dr. Joseph Murphy

33.	21st Century – Wayne Dyer – Eckhart Tolle – The Secret Speakers

Many more people could be included in this chronology as this is a short and generalized list.

Select Author or Teacher Biographies

Biographies of Select Authors who have focused on: Human Potential, Self-Help, Inspiration, Personal Development, Self- Improvement, New Thought, Metaphysics, and Mind Sciences.

Wallace D. Wattles (1860-1911)

Wattles was an American author and success writer. His most famous work was *The Science of Getting Rich*, or otherwise known as: *Financial Success Through Creative Thought*. He did profess to study thinkers such as Descartes, Spinoza, Leibnitz, Schopenhauer, Hegel, and Emerson. Wattles has positively affected millions with his books and philosophy of Mind Sciences or New Thought. His other books, including *The Science of Being Great*, have some excellent commentary and mind exercises for metaphysical wholeness and health.

Dr. Charles F. Haanel (1866-1949)

Haanel wrote the *Master Key System* in the early 1900s, which sold over two-hundred-thousand copies by 1933. It originally had twenty-four parts. The book is devoted to mind development and achieving your life's dreams using applied metaphysics. Charles F. Haanel was an American author, millionaire, entrepreneur, and businessman who belonged to several Freemason-related societies: the American Scientific League, The Author's

League of America, The American Society of Psychical Research, the St. Louis Humane Society, and the St. Louis Chamber of Commerce. *The Master Key System* is one of the classic studies in self-improvement, mind sciences, New Thought, and higher consciousness.

Robert Collier (1885– 1950)

Collier was an famous author of metaphysical books and self- improvement books in the twentieth century. Collier was born in St. Louis and was the nephew of the founder of *Collier's* magazine. He was involved in writing, editing, and research for most of his life. His book, *The Secret of the Ages*, sold over 300,000 copies during his life. Collier wrote about the practical psychology of abundance, desire, faith, visualization, confident action, and becoming your best. Robert Collier Publications, Inc., still exists through the efforts of his widow and now his children and grandchildren. Collier's books have recently been brought back to prominence from being referenced in the popular metaphysical movie, *The Secret*. Moreover, Robert Collier's books have been popular with self-help schools of thought and the Unity School of Christianity.

Prentice Mulford (1834-1891)

Prentice Mulford was an author, New Thought visionary, and adventurer. Born in Sag Harbor, Long Island, he sailed to San Francisco on a clipper in 1856 and remained for sixteen years. He left for a long tour of Europe in 1872 and then settled in New York City, where he became known as a comic lecturer and author of poems and essays and a columnist for the

New York Daily Graphic (a serial), 1875-1881. He may have founded the popular philosophy known as New Thought.

Life by Land and Sea (1889) contains Mulford's adventures at sea and in the West (1856-1872), life on a clipper and a California coastal schooner hunting whales and seals, gold prospecting in Tuolumne County, accounts of camp life, and experiences as a school teacher and minor local politician, copper mining in Stanislaus County, and his career as journalist for the *San Francisco Golden Era*.

Dr. JOSEPH MURPHY, PHD, DRS, LL.D., (1898-1981)

Murphy lectured to hundreds of thousands of people all over the world for nearly fifty years on the powers of the subconscious mind and Spiritual abundance. Born in 1898, he was educated in Ireland and England. Years of research studying the world's major religions convinced him that some great Power lay behind them all: The Power is within you!

Dr. Murphy was Founder/Minister-Director of the Church of Religious/Divine Science in Los Angeles for twenty-eight years, where his lectures were attended by over a thousand people almost every Sunday. He wrote over thirty books, including *The Amazing Laws of Cosmic Mind*, *The Miracle of Mind Dynamics*, *Your Infinite Power to Be Rich*, *Secrets of the I-Ching*, and *The Cosmic Power Within You* and also the famous *The Power of Your Subconscious Mind*. It is claimed that Murphy was influenced by Troward and Fox.

Dr. Christian D. Larson

Larson was a famous New Thought leader and teacher as well as a prolific author of metaphysical and New Thought books in the early 1900s. Larson's writings affected many great teachers and founders of several religions and philosophies.

Larson was honorary president of the International New Thought Alliance. Moreover, he was a colleague of with such notables as W.W. Atkinson, Horatio Dresser, Charles Brodie Patterson, and Annie Rix Militz. Moreover, his teachings greatly affected the life of Religious Science founder, Ernest Holmes, in his early career. Holmes had been studying the Christian Science textbook but came upon the writings of Larson. According to sources he steered away his earlier loyalties toward Larson's teachings.

Jesus Christ - 0 BCE to 33 AD.

We reference Jesus Christ as his teachings and word have inspired most of the authors analyzed and discussed herein.

Buddha

Siddhārtha Gautama (Pali, Gotama Buddha) - a Spiritual teacher from ancient India who founded Buddhism. He is universally recognized by Buddhists as the Supreme Buddha. The time of his birth and death are approximately 563 BCE to 483 BCE, though some have suggested a later date.

The foundation of Buddhist philosophy may include: The Four Noble Truths: that suffering is an inherent part of existence, that the origin of suffering is ignorance and the main symptoms of that ignorance are attachment and craving, that attachment and craving can be ceased, and that following the Noble Eightfold Path will lead to the cessation of attachment and craving and therefore suffering.

The Noble Eightfold Path includes: right understanding, right thought, right speech, right action, right livelihood, right effort, right mindfulness, and right concentration.

Dr. Thomas Troward (1847-1916)

Troward authored many books that are considered classics in the area of New Thought, Mind Sciences, and even mystic Christianity. Influences on his writings include the teachings of Christ, Islam, Hindu Teachings, Buddhism, and more. Troward was born in Punjab, India, educated in England, and received honors in literature. Thomas Troward was appointed Her Majesty's Assistant Commissioner and later Divisional Judge of the North Indian Punjab from 1869 until his retirement in 1896. He was a prize-winning artist and loved to research and write. Troward was raised in the Church of England but was extremely well educated in the religions and philosophies of the world. Troward was the author of many successful books including the famous: *Edinburgh Lectures 1904* and *Dore Lectures*. Troward's writings have influenced many great authors and religious leaders such as: Emmet Fox, Ernest Holmes, Paul Foster Case, Joseph Murphy, and even recent authors such as Bob Proctor. His contributions to the development of the New Thought Movement, human potential research, and Religious Science continue in the present day. His writings are sometimes very intellectual, but his grasp on a fusion of Eastern and Western philosophy is intense and make for fruitful readings.

Because Troward did not see a need for the occult, his writings challenged dogma in favor of a personal and abundant relationship with the Universal Spirit similar to the philosophy of Pierre Teilhard de Chardin or other great recent mystics. Troward spoke several languages, studied biblical scripture written in Hebrew, read the Koran, and researched the writings of Raja Yoga. Several of his books are in the public domain due to their publication before the 1920's.

Dr. Napoleon Hill (1883–1970)

At a fairly young adult, Hill was commissioned by Andrew Carnegie, one of the most wealthy men in the world at the time, to produce a successful compilation of the best practices of millionaires. Hill interviewed many of the most wealthy and famous people alive at the time including Thomas Edison, Alexander Graham Bell, George Eastman, Henry Ford, Elmer Gates, William Jennings Bryan, Theodore Roosevelt, John D. Rockefeller, Charles M. Schwab, F.W. Woolworth, William Wrigley Jr., John Wanamaker, William H. Taft, Woodrow Wilson, Charles Allen Ward, and Jennings Randolph. The research and writing of *Think and Grow Rich* lasted over twenty years. Ultimately, Hill sold over thirty-million books. As for his personal influences, he did write a letter to Charles F. Haanel to say that Haanel's *Master Key System* had much inspired him and changed his life.   Throughout his life, he spent a great deal of time teaching and helping others to learn the laws of success.

Other great books by Napoleon Hill are *Think and Grow Rich* (ISBN 1-59330-200-2), *How to Sell Your Way through Life* (ISBN 0-910882-11-8), *The Law of Success* (ISBN 0-87980-447-5).

Success Through a Positive Mental Attitude (ISBN 1-55525-270-2), *You Can Work Your Own Miracles* (ISBN 0-449-91177-2), and *Napoleon Hill's Keys to Success* (ISBN 0-452-27281-5).

James Allen

Allen was born in Leicester, England in 1864. James was 15 when his father, **a** businessman, was murdered. He left school **to** work full time to help support the family. Eventually married and became an executive secretary for a large corporation. At age 38, he retired from employment and he and his wife moved to a small cottage on the southwest shore of England to pursue a simple life of contemplation. There he wrote for 9 years producing over 20 works. James Allen died in 1912 at age 48.

A philosophical writer of United Kingdom or British nationality. James Allen's books illustrate the power of thought to have immense capabilities. Allen never achieved great fame or wealth, his works continue to influence people around the world. Allen's most famous book, *As a Man Thinketh* was published in 1902.

Dr. William Walker Atkinson (1862-1932)

Atkinson wrote a multitude of books on New Thought by various names. He wrote nearly a hundred books with many other pseudonyms: Theodore Sheldon, Theron Q.Dumont, Swami Panchadasi, The Three Initiates, Magus Incognitus

Originally from Maryland, he married and later became interested in Mental Science and Hinduism. He was admitted to practice as a lawyer in Pennsylvania and Illinois. Around 1916, he began writing articles for Elizabeth Towne's magazine The Nautilus, and from 1916 to 1919 Atkinson edited the journal Advanced Thought, and for a time honorary president of the International New Thought Alliance.

Dr. Orison Swett Marden 1850 - 1924

Marden was born in Thornton Gore, New Hampshire to Lewis and Martha Marden. When he was three years old, his mother died at the age of 22. When Orison was seven years old, his father died and he had to support himself from that point on. Inspired by a self-help book by the Scottish author Samuel Smiles, which he found in an attic, Marden determined to improve himself and his future. Marden succeeded in graduating from Boston University in 1871. He later graduated from Harvard with a M.D. in 1881 and an LL.B. degree in 1882. He also studied at the Boston School of Oratory and Andover Theological Seminary. Like many proponents of the New Thought philosophy, Marden believed that our thoughts influence our lives and our life circumstances. He said, "We make the world we live in and shape our own environment. He authored many books which include: Pushing to the Front or, Success Under Difficulties. 1894. How to Succeed or, Stepping-Stones to Fame and Fortune. 1896, Prosperity - How to Attract It. 1922.

Prof. Ralph Waldo Emerson (1803-1882)

Emerson is said to be the father of the American Renaissance. As he grew up in Boston, Emerson lived a difficult life with illness, poverty, and survived the death of his father when he was only 8 years old. His mother managed to raise 5 children alone, including one who was mentally challenged. At age 14, Emerson with the help of grants attended Harvard undergrad. After graduation, he taught at a girls school. Later, he returned to Harvard Divinity School. In 1829, after marrying Ellen Tucker, he was ordained a Unitarian minister. In 1831, his wife died, and he resigned from ministerial duties. He set off to Europe and Eurasia to seek and find himself. In 1835, having returned to the USA, Emerson married again to Lydia Jackson. In Concord, Massachusetts, they raised four children while Emerson gave Lectures and wrote poetry and prose combining his likes of philosophy and nature with politics. He was at the center of the American Transcendentalist movement. Emerson's major philosophy was that man and nature are the "essential perfectibility of the human spirit" and thought the ultimate meaning of life was the unity of the human soul with the divine oversoul. Emerson believed in "non conformity, creativeness, intellectual and spiritual independence, and self reliance." His contemporaries were among the likes of Henry Thoreau, Walt Whitman and Margaret Fuller. As a note, Emerson and William James did write essays and comment on Swedenborg. It seems that Swedenborg and Emerson did heavily influence the New Thought, Mind Science and other movements.

Dr. Ernest Shurtleff Holmes 1887-1960

Holmes was the founder of a movement known as Religious Science, also known as "Science of Mind," a part of the New Thought Movement. He is well known as the author of "The Science of Mind" and numerous other metaphysical books, and as the founder of Science of Mind magazine, in continuous publication since 1927. His books, radio broadcasts, and recordings continue to reach an audience of several hundred thousands of people world-wide, and the principles he taught as his Science of Mind have inspired and influenced many generations of metaphysical students and teachers. His influence beyond New thought can be see in the self-help movement.

Holmes wrote numerous books of theology, influenced by not only Emma Curtis Hopkins but also by Phineas Quimby, Thomas Troward, Ralph Waldo Emerson, various other New Thought writers of his day, and the texts of world religions. He came to prominence as a lecturer in the Los Angeles area, but ultimately formed a religious denomination now known as the United Church of Religious Science. Religious Science, like many New Thought faiths, emphasizes positive thinking, control of circumstances through mental processes, recognition of a creative energy (referred to as God, First Principle, Universal Intelligence, and other terms) that manifests as the physical universe, and the rejection of a good/evil duality.

Rev. Warren Felt Evans (1817-1889)

Evans was the son of a farmer and born to Eli and Sarah Edson Evans at Rockingham, Vermont, on December 23, 1817. Evans was one of 7 children. He studied at Chester Academy and in 1837 and later entered Middlebury College. In 1838, Evans transferred to Dartmouth College at Hanover, New Hampshire but left in the middle of his junior year to become a Methodist-Episcopal minister. He was married to M. Charlotte Tinker in 1840, and continued his Methodist ministry. In 1863, he left that church and joined the Church of the New Jerusalem (Swedenborgian). Evans wrote the first effective literature of New Thought. Scholars note that Evans's intellectual contribution to New Thought was to ground its practices in both the New Testament framework with the philosophies of Aristotle, Plato, Plotinus, Descartes, Liebniz, Fichte, Schelling, Berkeley, Spencer, Kant, Goethe, Emerson, Coleridge, Schleiermacher, even Kabbalah, Buddhist and Hindu thought, and especially Swedenborg. Furthermore, he had already been influenced by Quimby and began to develop his own insights on Mental Healing. Books by Evans include: The Mental Cure, Mental Medicine, The Divine Law of Cure, Esoteric Christianity and Mental Therapeutics, and others.

About George Mentz

Commissioner George Mentz is a premier, sought-after speaker, revolutionary author, and global management consultant. Dr. Mentz is universally referenced by his clientele, friends and colleagues as one of the most thoughtful, enthusiastic and empathetic leaders in the business world today. George Mentz, an international lawyer and passionate professor, is the founder of the GAFM Global Academy of Financial Management® and he has published extensively in the fields of law, e-business, SEO, entrepreneurship, marketing, international finance, and success strategy. George Mentz has advised and consulted with the US Government, United Nations and Fortune 500 companies on domestic and international strategy while helping people from around the world improve their education and careers.

George Mentz and his companies have held seminars and VIP courses in over 35 countries worldwide. Professor Mentz received his Doctor of Jurisprudence and MBA degrees after attending legal and business coursework at Loyola University, Université catholique Belgium, William and Mary Law School, Tulane University in the USA, Austria, Spain, Mexico and Brazil. Mentz is the first person in the United States to achieve "Quad Designation" Status as a JD, MBA, qualified/licensed financial planner and wealth manager, and Qualified/Certified Financial Consultant and Planner. Counselor Mentz is the recipient of national awards and honors for his contributions in the fields of management, excellence, teaching, charity, leadership and speaking. In recent years, George Mentz has been named an expert and leader for his publications and he has been honored by mainstream media as a brain trust member and part of the Dream Team of Financial Writers for mainstream media outlets. George Mentz has served on the advisory boards of: the Global Finance Forum in Switzerland, the World E-Commerce Forum in the UK, the Certified Economist Association of Africa, and the China Wealth Management Institute of Hong Kong, the Arab Academy Standards Council, the International Project Management Commission, a US medical school, a law school's Graduate Program, and various charities. Mentz is a syndicated author and two-time national award-winning professor, and is a contributor and expert for various organizations where some of Dr. Mentz's bestselling books and publications include: *CWM Chartered Wealth Manager Guide*, *Project Manager Executive Guide*, "Internet College Recruiting and Marketing", *The Wealth Management Executive Guide*, Online Credibility in the Finance World – Protecting Your Web Reputation & Company Brand, *The Secret Powers of Highly Effective People*, *Spiritual Wealth Management*, *Wealth Management and Financial Planning*, and many more. Published in many journals, Mentz is a pioneer in the movements of: executive certification training, international wealth management, internet marketing and human-potential through neuroplasticity. Mentz and his executive development companies are accredited by the TUV Austria, ISO Certified for Quality, and have been featured or quoted in the NASDAQ News, *Forbes*, *Reuters*, *Morningstar*, Yahoo Finance, *Wall Street Globe*, the *Hindu National*, *El Norte* Latin America, the *Financial Times*, *NYSSA New York Securities Analysts News*, the *ChinaDaily*, the Department of Education ERIC Library, the US Department of Labor Brochures, *Black Enterprise*, the *San Francisco Chronicle*, *Associated Press* and the *Arab Times*.

http://www.GeorgeMentz.com

You can contact Dr.jur. GS Mentz at his website, www.gmentz.com on Linkedin.com at https://www.linkedin.com/in/georgementz

---

[i] Wikipedia - http://en.wikipedia.org/wiki/New_Thought_Movement

[ii] A History of the New Thought Movement- by Horatio W. Dresser, published by Thomas Y. Crowell Co., New York, 1919

[iii] Martin Luther and Swedenborg http://en.wikipedia.org/wiki/Swedenborg

[iv] A History of the New Thought Movement- by Horatio W. Dresser, published by Thomas Y. Crowell Co., New York, 1919, Chapter 6

[v] Biography of Judge Thomas Troward – www.thomastroward.wwwhubs.com

---

[vi] The Secret - http://www.amazon.com/Secret-Rhonda-Byrne/dp/1582701709

[vii] Smiles, S. (2002). *Self-Help: With Illustrations of Character, Conduct, and Perseverance. Oxford, UK: Oxford University Press.* Samuel Smiles - http://en.wikipedia.org/wiki/Samuel_Smiles

[viii] O. S. Marden - http://en.wikipedia.org/wiki/Orison_Swett_Marden

[ix] Christian Larson http://en.wikipedia.org/wiki/Christian_Larson or http://christianlarson.wwwhubs.com

[x] Hill, N. (1960). *Think and Grow Rich*, New York: Fawcett Crest.

[xi] Mulford, Prentice (1908). *Thoughts are Things Essays Selected From The White Cross Library.* Location: Publisher.

[xii] Collier, R. (1970). *Be Rich.* Oak Harbor, WA: Robert Collier Publishing.

[xiii] Troward, Judge Thomas (1904). *The Edinburgh Lectures on Mental Science.* Location: Publisher.

[xiv] Haanel, Mentz (2006). *How to Master Abundance and Prosperity - The* Master Key System *Decoded.* Location: Xlibris Pub.

[xv] Ibid.

[xvi] Master Key System (28 Part Complete Deluxe Edition) - Ishtar Publishing (July 2007) ISBN 978-0-9780535-8-1

[xvii] **W. W. Atkinson**. Secret of Success: Self-Healing by Thought Force. 1907

[xviii] **W. W. Atkinson**. Law of the New Thought: A Study of Fundamental Principles & Their Application. 1902.

[xix] Murphy, J. (2002). *The Power of Your Subconscious Mind*, New York: Bantam Books.

[xx] Allen, J. (1998). *As You Think.* Ed. with introduction by M. Allen. Novato, CA: New World Library

[xxi] Ibid.

[xxii] *The Ideal Made Real: or, Applied Metaphysics for Beginners* (Chicago: The Progress

---

Company, 1909), by Christian D. Larson

[xxiii] Ibid.

[xxiv] Wattles, W.D. (1976). *Financial Success through the Power of Thought* [*The Science of Getting Rich*]. Rochester, Vermont: Destiny Books. (Written originally around 1910).

[xxv] Ibid.

[xxvi] Beatitudes - Matthew 5:2-10 - NIV translation

[xxvii] Ibid.

[xxviii] *Alcoholics Anonymous : the story of how many thousands of men and women have recovered from alcoholism.* 4th ed. New York : Alcoholics Anonymous World Services, 2001. ISBN 1893007162.

[xxix] Masters of the Secrets, Mentz Publishing, 2007 Mentz, Pages 192-193

[xxx] The Science of Being Great" by Wattles – Elizabeth Towne Publishing 1914

- Excerpts, paragraphs, and selected content in this book are from pre-1925 writings of: Wallace Wattles, Christian Larson, William Walker Atkinson, and Genevieve Behrend

---

Other References or Authors of Interest

Allen, J. (1998). *As You Think*. Ed. with introduction by M. Allen. Novato, CA: New World Library

Behrend, G. (1927) Your Invisible Power. Montana: Kessinger Publishing.

Carnegie, D. (1994). *How to Win Friends and Influence People*. New York: Pocket Books. http://www.dalecarnegie.com

Carlson, R. (2001). *Don't Sweat the Small Stuff About Money*. Location: Hyperion. Previously published as *Don't Worry Make Money* http://www.dontsweat.com.

Chopra, D. (1996). *The Seven Spiritual Laws of Success*. London: Bantam Press. http://www.chopra.com

Collier, R. (1970). *Be Rich*. Oak Harbor, WA: Robert Collier Publishing. http://robertcollierpublications.com

Covey, S. R. (1989). *The 7 Habits of Highly Effective People*. London: Simon & Schuster. http://www.stephencovey.com

Dyer, W. (1993). *Real Magic: Creating Miracles in Everyday Life*. New York: HarperCollins. http://www.drwaynedyer.com

Gawain, Shakti (1979). *Creative Visualization*. Mill Valley: Publisher. http://www.shaktigawain.com

Haanel, Mentz (2006). *How to Master Abundance and Prosperity - The* Master Key System *Decoded*. Location: Xlibris Pub.

Carlson Haanel Wattles, Mentz (2005). *The Science of Growing Rich*. Location: Xlibris Publishing.

Hill, N. (1960). *Think and Grow Rich*, New York: Fawcett Crest.

His Holiness the Dalai Lama & Howard C. Cutler (1999). *The Art of Happiness: A handbook for Living*. London: Hodder & Stroughton. http://www.dalailama.com

James, William (1902). *The Varieties of Religious Experience*. Location: Publisher.

Maltz, Maxwell, MD. Psycho-Cybernetics. New York. Pocket Books 1960

Marden, O. S. (1997). *Pushing to the Front, or Success under Difficulties*, Vols 1 & 2. Santa Fe, CA: Sun Books.

Mentz, G. S. (2006) *Other Books and Summaries on The Secrets of Life and Abundance:* http://gmentz.com

Mulford, Prentice (1908). *Thoughts are Things - Essays Selected From The White Cross Library*. Location: Publisher.

Murphy, J. (1963). *The Power of Your Subconscious Mind*, New Jersey: Prentice Hall.

Ponder, C. (1962) *The Dynamic Laws of Prosperity*, Camarillo, CA: DeVorss & Co.

Roman & Packer (1988). *Creating Money*: Tiburon, CA: Kramer. http://www.orindaben.com

Price, J. R. (1987). *The Abundance Book*. Carlsbad, CA: Hay House. http://www.johnrandolphprice.com

Smiles, S. (2002). *Self-Help: With Illustrations of Character, Conduct, and Perseverance. Oxford, UK: Oxford University Press.*

Tracy, B. (1993). *Maximum Achievement: Strategies and Skills That Will Unlock Your Hidden Powers to Succeed.* New York: Fireside. http://www.briantracy.com

Troward, Judge Thomas (1904). *The Edinburgh Lectures on Mental Science.* Location: Publisher.

Wattles, W.D. (1976). *Financial Success through the Power of Thought* [*The Science of Getting Rich*]. Rochester, Vermont: Destiny Books. (Written originally around 1910).

Wilkinson, Bruce (2000). *The Prayer of Jabez.* City, OR: Multnamah Publishers. http://www.prayerofjabez.com

Bibliography

Other References or Authors of Interest

Allen, J. (1998). *As You Think.* Edited with an introduction by M. Allen. Novato, CA: New World Library.

Aurelius, M. (1964) *Meditations*, trans. M. Staniforth, London: Penguin.

The Bhagavad-Gita (1973) trans. J. Mascaró, London: Penguin World's Classics..

Behrend, G. (1927) *Your Invisible Power.* Montana: Kessinger Publishing.

Carnegie, D. (1994). *How to Win Friends and Influence People.* New York: Pocket Books.

Carlson, R. (2001). *Don't Sweat the Small Stuff About Money.* New York, USA: Hyperion.

Chopra, D. (1996). *The Seven Spiritual Laws of Success.* London: Bantam Press.

Collier, R. (1970). *Be Rich.* Oak Harbor, Washington: Robert Collier Publishing.

Coelho, P. (1999) *The Alchemist*, trans. Alan R Clarke, London: HarperCollins.

Covey, S. R. (1989). *The 7 Habits of Highly Effective People.* London: Simon & Schuster.

Dyer, W. (1993). *Real Magic: Creating Miracles in Everyday Life.* New York: HarperCollins.

Eker, T. H. (2005). *Secrets of the Millionaire Mind: Mastering the Inner Game of Wealth.* New York: HarperCollins Publishers.

Emerson, R.W. (1993) *Self-Reliance*, Dover Publications.

Gawain, Shakti (1979). *Creative Visualization.* New World Library, Mill Valley USA.

Bishop Bernard Jordan (2007). The Laws of Thinking: 20 Secrets to Using the Divine Power of Your Mind to Manifest Prosperity." (2007) *(9781401917968): Published by Hay House and Bishop E. Bernard Jordan: Books*

Hill, N. (1960). *Think and Grow Rich*. New York: Fawcett Crest.

His Holiness the Dalai Lama, with H. C. Cutler (1999). *The Art of Happiness: A Handbook for Living.* London: Hodder & Stroughton.

James, W. (1902). *The Varieties of Religious Experience.* Longman Publishing, London, UK.

Jeffers, S. (1991) Feel the Fear and Do It Anyway, London: Arrow Books.

Lao-Tzu's Tao Te Ching (2000) trans. T. Freke, introduction by M. Palmer, London: Piatkus.

Maltz, M.. (1960). *Psycho-Cybernetics.* New York. Pocket Books.

Marden, O. S. (1997). *Pushing to the Front, or Success under Difficulties,* Vols. 1–2. Santa Fe, California: Sun Books.

Mentz, C. W. H. (2007). *Masters of the Secrets: And the Science of Getting Rich and Master Key System Expanded: Bestseller Version.* Bloomington, Indiana, United States: Xlibris Corp.

Mentz, C. W. H. (2006). *How to Master Abundance and Prosperity—The Master Key System Decoded.* Bloomington Indiana: Xlibris Pub.

Mentz, C. W. H. (2005). *The Science of Growing Rich.* Bloomington, Indiana: Xlibris Publishing.

Mentz, George S - *Other Books by Mentz.* http://www.lulu.com/gmentz

---

Mulford, P. (1908). *Thoughts Are Things: Essays Selected from the White Cross Library.* G. Bell and Sons, Ltd., LONDON, 1908.

Murphy, J. (1963). *The Power of Your Subconscious Mind.* New Jersey: Prentice Hall.

Peale, N.V. (1996) *The Power of Positive Thinking,* New York: Ballantine Books.

Ponder, C. (1962). *The Dynamic Laws of Prosperity.* Camarillo, California: DeVorss & Co.

Price, J. R. (1987). *The Abundance Book.* Carlsbad, California: Hay House.

Roman, S., Packer, D. R. (2008). Creating Money: *Attracting Abundance.* Tiburon, California: H. J. Kramer, Inc., published in a joint venture with New World Library.

Scovell Shinn, F. (1998) *The Game of Life and How to Play It,* Saffron Walden: C.W. Daniel.

Seicho-no Iye (生長の家). Books by Dr. Masaharu Taniguchi.

Smiles, S. (2002). *Self-Help: With Illustrations of Character, Conduct, and Perseverance.* Oxford: Oxford University Press.

Thoreau, H.D. (1986) *Walden and Civil Disobedience,* introduction by M. Meyer, New York: Penguin.

Tracy, B. (1993). *Maximum Achievement: Strategies and Skills That Will Unlock Your Hidden Powers to Succeed.* New York: Fireside.

Troward, T. (1904). *The Edinburgh Lectures on Mental Science.* DODD, MEAD & COMPANY: New York.

Wattles, W. D. (1976). *Financial Success through the Power of Thought: The Science of Getting Rich.* Rochester, Vermont: Destiny Books.

Wilkinson, B. (2000). *The Prayer of Jabez.* Colorado Springs, CO USA, OR: Multnamah Publishers.

---

the philosophy of Professor Wattles, Behrend, Larson, Atkinson, and some others as seen in the citations. From the dark ages to the Reformation and Enlightenment, the world began to study, interpret, and deliver the universal truth, secrets of prosperity and peace of mind. Much of the content included is analysis, commentary and expanded insights related to Wattles, with a section referencing Thomas Troward and his pupil G. Behrend's work, along with some content from Emerson.